Aliza shares real stories in a fresh, original and relatable manner. And they add up to great advice on how you can make the most of your career.

– Claire Hughes Johnson,
COO, Stripe

Don't Quit Your Day Job is an inspiring, engaging, and essential read on how to be the best you can be in life and your career. Aliza provides her uniquely human, practical and honest insights into what can help you achieve your full potential, drawing on her rich career and experiences to provide pragmatic ways to successfully respond to the many challenges of becoming a great leader.

– David Thodey,
Chair, Xero and Tyro; former Chair, CSIRO;
former CEO, Telstra

This is the best career advice I've read. Follow it and you will enjoy your life and work, and excel in what matters to you. Aliza brings her extensive senior global experience across a range of industries to help readers work out what they want and how to get it. It answers every question I've ever been asked by people seeking career direction and advice. Wish I'd written it.

– Margie Seale,
Non-Executive Director, Scentre Group and Westpac;
former CEO, Random House Australia and New Zealand

When I started my career at BCG 30 years ago, Aliza Knox taught me some of the principles that got me to where I am today. In *Don't Quit Your Day Job*, you'll learn them too. Her advice is priceless.

– Brad Banducci,
CEO Woolworths Group

Don't Quit Your Day Job provides practical tips and advice for success in your career. Aliza Knox distils her vast experience as a global business leader and mentor to highlight the mindshifts you need to expand your career opportunities and build your success at any stage of your life.

– Dig Howitt,
CEO and President, Cochlear Ltd

Good people are hard to find and keeping them is even harder. *Don't Quit Your Day Job* will show individuals how they can get the most from where they are, and give managers the tips and tools to keep their talent from moving on.

– Alison Deitz,
Chief Executive Partner, Norton Rose Fulbright Australia

Your career can take you anywhere. This highly readable and relatable book by Aliza Knox, *Don't Quit Your Day Job*, is an inspiration for how to make your career and your life work for you.

– Alison Davis,
Managing Partner, Blockchain Coinvestors

don't quit *your* day job

***The* 6 mindshifts you need to *Rise* and *Thrive* at work**

don't quit *your* day job

Aliza Knox *with* Wendy Paris

WILEY

First published in 2022 by John Wiley & Sons Australia, Ltd

42 McDougall St, Milton Qld 4064
Office also in Melbourne

Typeset in KazimirText 10pt/14pt

ISBN: 978-0-730-39659-8

A catalogue record for this book is available from the National Library of Australia

Cover design by Wiley

SKY761E7000-CE8C-43E5-BAE9-79A039A89D94_031422

Contents

Letter to the reader

If you have a job or are seeking one, this book is for you. While the conversation in the media or even at a dinner party might be about entrepreneurship or exploiting your 'side hustle' or 'the great resignation', the day-to-day reality is that most of us work for someone else, and, increasingly, in large organisations. We also work for decades, which may sound daunting (and exhausting), but as you'll see in this book, plenty of people find ways to make work rewarding, fulfilling and, dare I say, *fun*.

Across the globe, an increasing percentage of people work for large companies. In the UK alone, nearly half of the workers are employed by firms with 250 people or more. In the US, as of the 2014 Census data, nearly 40 per cent of workers were employed at either large companies (those with 2500 people or more),[1] or very large ones (with 10 000 people or more).[2] Close to another third of workers in the US were at mid-sized companies (with 100 to 2500 employees).

As corporations and businesses continue to grow, so will opportunities within them. What you need to succeed are the six mindshifts laid out as chapters in this book. The mindshifts are outlined, then brought to life with relatable examples of people I've met along the way. All of these people are real, though some names, and occasionally some genders, have been changed – as they used to say on TV – 'to protect the innocent'. Ways to put the mindshifts into practice are listed at the end of each chapter so you can adopt the ones that work for you.

***

If my life had worked out differently, I might have been a forester – planting trees, assessing timber plots – and writing about it all in a rough-hewn log cabin surrounded by towering redwoods, with the occasional bear ambling by.

This wasn't actually a dream of mine as a child; growing up in the US, I had no specific vision of what my career would be. I worked odd jobs to earn and save money in high school, and one of these jobs involved taking aptitude and personality tests at Stanford University's Graduate School of Education. One test indicated that I'd be well-suited to a life in forestry or the clergy.

Neither option, I confess, interested me remotely.

I wasn't really exposed to people working within large corporations, and I never particularly thought about corporate life either. I've now spent the past 40 years working for, and leading, businesses at some of the world's most interesting, innovative companies – including more than a decade heading the Asia Pacific (APAC) region for parts of Google, as well as for Twitter and Cloudflare. Before that, I served as the first female partner in Asia at Boston Consulting Group (BCG). Over the years, I also had roles in the financial services sector, including at Visa, American Express and Charles Schwab.

I went to Brown University, where you didn't have to declare a major until your junior year, which was one reason I chose the school. After graduating with a degree in applied math and economics, I took a job in banking because it ticked two boxes on my wish list: a great training program, and the opportunity to move to New York City, which seemed like an exciting place to live.

While much of my career has been in sales and general management, these were not early interests. As a teen, I subscribed to *Seventeen* magazine (typical) and *Psychology Today* (oddball choice), thinking that maybe I'd become a psychologist. I had exactly one early experience in sales, creating an ad book with three friends in high school to fund our senior year activities. I had to go to dozens of merchants I didn't know and ask for money to advertise to the students and parents. It was my idea and I persisted with it. Looking back now, that is the real through-line in my career – perseverance. Once I decide on something, I'm full steam ahead, driven to make it happen. Recently, my mom said that even in high school I was always tired because I was trying to cram in one more thing.

It's easy to feel like you should know exactly what you want to do in your career in order to be successful and happy, to have a specific vision and then execute it. But that hasn't been my path, or that of many of the people in this book. The fact is, you don't have to know what you want to do to rise and thrive, and even if you do know now, you may change your mind later. Today's rapid pace of change means that many of the most exciting fields and companies of the future probably don't exist now. Even if you love what you're doing, something else might arise that intrigues you (as the Internet did for me in my forties). Even though I didn't have a specific plan in mind (other than travel; I knew I wanted to travel), I did have drive, curiosity and a desire to connect and help out. These traits have helped me, and embracing them can help you, too.

People who look at my career from the outside and see me as super-successful sometimes conclude that success must mean never failing. But this isn't true either. While I love helping build businesses, and am proud of my achievements, I've also had my share of missteps, including twice taking jobs that I quickly regretted and left in less than a year. I've been laid off; once my department was dissolved, and I had to let go of my whole team, and then leave myself.

Success doesn't require an early, clear-cut vision, nor does it come from never having setbacks. Rather, it grows from working hard and adopting some crucial mindsets or *mindshifts* – attitudes you can learn, and put into practice.

Over the past 40 years, I've come to identify six essential *mindshifts* made by those who succeed; six powerful attitudes and actions that underpin organisational success. I have watched people thrive using these mindsets. I've also seen other very smart, talented people fail to flourish because they didn't embrace them. These are the mindsets I want to share with you in this book.

Success means something different to different people, of course. For you, it might mean achieving a certain lifestyle, or rising to a desired position or reputation within an industry. It could mean fame and fortune, influence, making a difference, helping others, or supporting a family comfortably. In my own life, success has meant having the lifestyle I want, achieving financial comfort sufficient for my family and some charitable giving, and rising to reasonably high positions, though not CEO. But I do also have a universal view of success, which includes having some sense of control over your life; feeling of agency in your career; and liking, for the most part, how you spend your time, who you spend it with, and how much you're earning. This is the view of success that this book can help you achieve.

I've also had a not-so-secret sideline occupation as a 'mentor maven', an unofficial (unpaid) career coach and supporter for hundreds of people at all stages of their working lives. Over the decades, I have listened to, and advised, people negotiating promotions and setbacks, struggling to rise and preserve time with their families, hoping to move overseas or return home, deciding whether to accept an offer or keep looking, and strategising about how to fight back when wronged.

The stories of some of these mentees are in this book, too. Helping other people develop has been the most fulfilling activity of my life, besides raising my own kids. Maybe having lacked the coordination (or popularity) required to be a cheerleader in high school left me with a desire to cheer on people in the career arena. Mentoring and advising people has brought me tremendous pride, and enabled me to gain more pleasure from working. If I didn't work, I wouldn't be able to help these people or forge these connections.

Sometimes people reach out for advice because I've long been one of the few female sales executives in the hardscrabble tech business. Others seek input because I'm older and have survived. Or because I'm more approachable than Tony Robbins or a celebrity CEO. People want to know how to find time to raise children and travel regularly for work, how to manage setbacks without letting them sap confidence and derail goals. This is another reason I'm writing this book: to take this mentoring to more people, to share with you what those I've mentored have learned.

After so many years in tech, I now see my career as a series of software upgrades. Aliza 1.0 was consulting and financial services; 2.0 was tech. What you're holding in your hands now is part of Aliza 3.0, the third iteration of my working life. I'm still experimenting with what I want to do, and this book is part of this third phase. It's a way to continue my greatest work passion: sharing lessons learned from decades of leading US companies across new frontiers while building and maintaining strong connections between teams around the world. In a world where 'remote workforce' defines more of us than ever before, this background allows me to offer insight and wisdom as a leader who has been in charge of far-flung workforces for years.

In many ways, now is the best time ever to be looking for a job or seeking a better one. It seems like you can't read the news without seeing an article about how much work is changing, both the structure within offices, and what people want and expect from their jobs. We are in a moment of real dynamism at work. Companies that once required everyone to be physically present at headquarters or in one of their offices around the globe are going remote or adopting hybrid models. Employees who never had the flexibility to work from home are now considering it, or even making it a condition of employment.

COVID-19 has forced, or allowed, people to re-evaluate their careers and values, their trajectory and even what a career path means for them. Nobel prize winner and *New York Times* columnist Paul Krugman summed up the general sentiment, 'It seems quite possible that the pandemic, by upending many Americans' lives, also caused some of them to reconsider their life choices.'[3]

In many fields, employers are scrambling to fill roles. The demand for workers affects everything from salary and bonuses to in-office perks, flexible work arrangements and even time off. This gives would-be employees leverage that didn't exist for most of my time at work.

Additionally, corporations, non-profits, government agencies and universities are investing resources in expanding the diversity of job candidates, employees and leaders, and rightly so. This opens exciting opportunities for many people who may have felt shut out of top jobs in the past, and is leading to an improved workplace.

Diversity also boosts the bottom line, an undeniable motivator for firms. Take gender diversity, as one example: a Peterson Institute for International Economics survey of nearly 20 000 firms operating in 91 countries found a repeated, demonstrable correlation between women at the C-suite level and higher profitability:

> ***... and the magnitude of the estimated effects is not small. For example, a profitable firm at which 30 percent of leaders are women could expect to add more than 1 percentage point to its net margin compared with an otherwise similar firm with no female leaders.*** [4]

Even if, in your own life, you've experienced the push for diversity as more talk than action, a more diverse workforce is absolutely the direction of the future.

***

Career success increasingly depends on working well with others within an organisation. For me, this book could also be called, *How to Succeed in Business by Being Your Best Self*. It describes a way of rising in your career that hinges on exhibiting the attributes we ascribe to being a good person, colleague and friend: being reliable and trustworthy, encouraging of others and making time for yourself.

This advice comes not only from my work experience, but also from my deep belief in the value of caring about others while also advocating for yourself; of seeing the world as full of opportunities, not a zero-sum-game; the options plentiful, not scarce. You can thrive in your career without adopting a narrow-eyed, cutthroat, winner-take-all approach. Yes, work is highly competitive, and you can't expect anyone else to look out for you, but you. A career is not a family; your boss doesn't love you like a good parent, and may not even like you. Your boss doesn't have to be your friend, but they do need to value the work you're doing and respect your contribution.

There certainly are people who are jerks and succeed. They have personal goals and they go after them; if they step on a few people along the way, that doesn't deter them. Nasty people can do well in business. As much as I'd like to believe that the people who climb on others are miserable at home, they may not be. Some may even be happy with their lives. But this overly self-focused approach to success is not mine, and not the vision of this book. (It is, however, one reason you need stamina, which I cover in chapter 2. Part of thriving is surviving, including being able to process unfairness and refocus on your own path.)

The strategy in this book is not about using others to get ahead. This is not Sun Tzu's *The Art of War*, nor Machiavelli's *The Prince*. It's an approach that involves being open and enthusiastic about work and those around you, learning the power structure within your place of business, making sure you find supporters at work and outside of your job, and being a mentor and supporter for those coming up after you. It's about making a choice and throwing yourself into it, getting out of a role or company if it becomes clear that you can't get ahead within it, and being flexible about your dreams. It advocates being open to the serendipity around you, the people you meet and the personal passions that are part of a full life.

The book could also, perhaps, be called, *Getting In and Staying In*. So many of these mindsets require stamina, and while chapter 2 focuses specifically on this attribute, as you'll see, a long, rewarding career requires being able to deal with setbacks, to refocus and continue to do what's needed to thrive.

***

The six mindshifts, in brief

I see the mindshifts in this book as timeless. They are based on my 40 years of work and of listening to and guiding people at all stages of their careers, from recent college grads and mid-career professionals to leaders within Fortune 100 firms. It includes my stories and those of numerous people who represent a wide range of backgrounds and professions. Each chapter ends with specific takeaways you can apply in your own life. The world of work is always changing, but these essential mindshifts remain the same.

Organisational life is appreciably better now for many than in the recent past. Piruze, who you meet in chapter 1, is an example of how people today are endeavouring to improve the work environment — and winning. She focused on doing an excellent job at work and at home, and designing a role that would not mean forfeiting the time she needed in either realm. As she discovered, thriving in both worlds is easier if you are very clear about what you want, present your desires to your boss professionally and clearly (backed by data, if you can find it), and remain flexible and willing to work with the firm to make it a success for everyone.

Stamina is a career superpower and, as I explain in chapter 2, stamina can be built. One important mindset to help build stamina: don't over-focus on the negative. Another: remember that you have options. As Mariabrisa discovered when she did some 'job dating' to see what other options might exist, her skills and experience were far more valuable in the marketplace than she knew.

In chapter 3, you will meet Rahul and learn why I offered him a job while we were walking through a revolving door together in Beijing (hint: we formed a bond while travelling). You will learn that connections with peers and leaders can be as significant as work performance when it comes to rising and thriving, and that arguably the most important capital you can accrue in business is not financial capital, but *social* capital.

Yet another story, of a man I call Bo, in chapter 4, shows in some cases how much things haven't changed in the world of work, despite today's focus on employee satisfaction, hybrid teams and diversity. You still will likely have experiences of being treated unfairly, and you have to fight back when you're wronged. No, this does not have to mean taking a firm to court, or even being rehired after an unjust termination. But it does mean standing up for yourself in a way that will let you move forward, and preserve your good relationship with your career.

In chapter 5, you will learn about how people are using movement to rise and thrive — not only moving up, as in preparing for and getting promotions, but also moving from one field to another, and between firms, industries and sectors. You'll also learn how to create movement where you are through 'job crafting', which a man I call Tim has done to redesign his current job to include more challenges and creative growth, culminating in higher job satisfaction.

And in chapter 6, you will see how Sierra's request to move to a company's overseas office expanded her professional opportunities and enhanced her personal life – even though she didn't wind up heading to her first dream destination. Like Sierra, your desire to move overseas can be a benefit to your company. Understanding and embracing the truly global nature of work today is key to succeeding and making the kinds of connections that help work feel meaningful.

We are all standing together at a unique, historic inflection point, a moment in which our beliefs about the future of work are shifting as rapidly as the technology we're using to make it happen. This change is exciting and challenging, and it requires a strong set of tools and a new outlook to succeed.

This book is that toolbox. Thank you for opening it and being part of the conversation. Here's to rising and thriving into the future, whatever it may bring.

mindshift one

Go for both: Your work and your life are on the same team

Power perspectives in this chapter

- embrace non-work passions
- make work fun
- don't agonise over decisions as there are very few truly wrong ones
- see the serendipity and act on it.

In 2007, after more than two decades of working in financial services and consulting — a journey that took me from Bankers Trust in New York City to BCG in Sydney and Singapore, and then to Charles Schwab and Visa in California — I did something radical. I made a mid-career switch that was risky. I took a lower title and a pay cut to move into a new industry that I didn't know much about: technology. I moved to Google to run APAC online sales (followed by leadership roles at Twitter and, most recently, Cloudflare, an internet security company).

Not long after I landed the job at Google, I travelled from my then-home in San Francisco to Sydney to introduce myself to the Australian team. While in Sydney, I met a young American woman named Suzy Nicoletti. Suzy was at the beginning of her career, and was bright and energetic. She seemed right at home in outdoorsy Sydney. We immediately bonded over a conversation about swimming. (It's kind of impossible *not* to talk about the water in Sydney, a harbour city with beaches.) Suzy had been a competitive swimmer in college in Los Angeles; I'm also an avid swimmer, though not at the collegiate level. We also talked about our favourite American foods that are unavailable in Asia (Stove Top Stuffing, Suzy; Diet Dr Pepper, me). Chatting about non-work interests like these helps reveal the human side of colleagues, and of yourself, making it a valuable part of having a career you love because it helps you create a work community filled with people you care about.

Over the next few years, Suzy would reach out occasionally to check in and update me about her career progress and goals. This is often how I become a mentor to someone; we'll meet through work or socially, and take the time to connect. Over time, Suzy began expressing a desire to step into a larger leadership role.

After five years at Google, I left to take another Singapore-based position: building APAC for Twitter. I needed someone to fill an important role running mid-market sales and operations in Australia. *This would be a great opportunity for Suzy Nicoletti!* The job had a lot of responsibility and would be a big promotion aligned with her career goals. I was excited to offer her the position.

But when I did, she turned me down.

How was this possible? How could she say no to a great role (and one that would let her work for a great boss, as in *me*, I might add)?

She wanted to have kids, she told me. From everything she'd heard about the demands of corporate leadership and of caring for a baby, she couldn't do both. She had to pick one or the other. Also, she wasn't sure she could handle the job.

I knew she could do the work, and that she could be a good leader *and* a great parent. I did not buy the idea that you could only have one or the other – I still don't – and I told her so.

I've never subscribed to that either-or limiting view, and I often feel like it's part of my personal mission to help others see beyond it. Not everyone wants a family, but I do believe everyone can have a great career and a fulfilling personal life. During several calls, I tried to steer Suzy toward taking the job. How could she give up before trying? Why let her desire to have a family slow her professional growth? During a turning-point conversation over lattes at a beach café in Sydney, she finally agreed to give it a shot.

She thrived in the position, *and* she had her baby. She went on to have a second child while still in that role. Within three years, she landed another promotion, this time as the managing director of Twitter, Australia/New Zealand.

I'm happy to report that her career and (now three) children are all doing well.

The 'Ah-Hah!' of Suzy's story: step off the seesaw of work-life balance

So many people I've met believe they'll come to an 'either-or' moment in their careers as Suzy did, a time when one of their most important desires will have to give way. They ask, 'Isn't it impossible to have a great career *and* a really fulfilling home life? Don't I have to sacrifice one for the other?'

No, you don't. Not in my experience, or in the experience of hundreds of people I've met and advised over the years. Yes, there are a lot of difficulties when you're trying to raise children and hold down a career, or practice your profession and pursue sport at a national level or work and be a full time career. It can be quite hard, and the difficulties the media points out are real.

There are trade-offs to be made, of course. You might not get as much sleep as you'd like all the time. Your house might not be as consistently clean as you wish. Your wardrobe might not be particularly stylish (I'm talking about myself here). You might push some limits occasionally (like flying from Singapore to Thailand for a meeting in a huge raincoat to hide from the airline-rule-bound flight attendants *just how pregnant* you are. Yes, me again). It can be expensive to manage with a modicum of calm. My husband and I definitely spent way more than we'd planned, or thought we could, on child care to accommodate both of our careers, and not everyone can afford that option.

Still, I've seen so many women and men rise in the corporate world, non-profit arena, government or academia while also having a full life outside of it – whether that means building a family or pursuing another personal passion. New Zealand's prime minister, Jacinda Ardern, is an inspiring, high-profile example of going for both. She had a baby while in office in 2018, and her partner, Clarke Gayford, stayed home to care for the baby. As she put it, 'I am not the first woman to multitask. I am not the first woman to work and have a baby; there are many women who have done this before.'

This helps send an important message: we can pursue our goals at work, and outside of it. In fact, Prime Minister Ardern is the second elected head of government to give birth in office, after Pakistan's late Prime Minister Benazir Bhutto. As Helen Clark, the former New Zealand prime minister and former head of the UN Development Programme, put it, 'For young women, the example Ardern is setting is an affirmation that they too can expect to have that choice'.[1]

In my own life, I have been able to hold leadership positions, and do the things that are important to me – rise in my career from an entry-level position at a bank in New York to leading teams distributed across Asia from Singapore for some of the top tech firms in the world – *and also* have a lot of fun with my husband, raise two sons, belong to three book groups, exercise and volunteer.

We've all heard the phrase 'work-life balance'. It sounds like a good goal, yet this formula suggests that work and life are at odds with each other, on opposite ends of a seesaw; one must be down for the other to be up. But our lives are not seesaws. They're more like cars, and we want all wheels filled to ensure a smooth, satisfying ride. We need to shift away from the constricting, adversarial model of 'your work *or* your life', and embrace a more expansive, inclusive, flexible vision. We can establish goals and drive toward them in *all* areas of our lives.

For some people, an expansive view includes not being tied to a specific job or title. Simon Kantor, a London-based, married father of two, has worked for a consultancy, the British Government, tech and communications firms (most recently as the chief operating officer), and today, is at Egon Zehnder, one of the top executive search firms in the world. While he's had high-powered, rewarding roles, he has structured his career to support his life as a whole and his family.

> ***Some people let their jobs define them, but for a lot of people, that's not the case. I don't define myself as a recruiter. I'm a father, a friend, a husband, a son. If I can add 'trusted advisor', I want to be that, too.***[2]

Simon takes something of a historical perspective to the question of the role of work. He sees himself as lucky, in general, to be able to pursue various opportunities, and to craft a life that he loves. 'I'm living a life my ancestors couldn't imagine', he says. 'To me, having health, good fortune and family is what matters. The work makes that possible.' (For more on Simon's varied career moves, see chapter 5.)

Anne-Marie Slaughter, CEO of the Washington DC–based think tank New America and author of several books, has written about how she realised that success in multiple domains can depend on paying attention to the *specifics* of each. Slaughter was working as the dean of Princeton University's Woodrow Wilson School of Public and International Affairs, living in New Jersey and raising two sons with her husband. In 2009, she took a two-year public service leave from the university for an incredibly prestigious (and time-consuming) position in Washington, DC, as the first female director of policy planning in the US State Department. This is one of the highest jobs in the State Department and it comes with huge responsibility and amazing opportunities. For Slaughter, it also came with having to leave her house to catch the 5.30 am train to DC every Monday, and being away from home until late Friday night.

Despite the amazing opportunities the job afforded, after two years, she decided it wasn't the right role, given her other life goals – which included being physically present for her two teenage sons at a time when they really needed her. She returned to Princeton, a decision made partly due to this realisation, and partly due to Princeton's policies around how long a professor can be absent before losing tenure (two years). 'I realized ... having it all, at least for me, depended almost entirely on what type of job I had', she writes.[3]

Back in Princeton, Slaughter continued with a busy, high-powered career of teaching, writing, giving speeches and doing TV appearances. Still, as she writes in a now-famous *Atlantic* article about the experience, some women her age and older were quick to label her decision as giving up, as being stymied by the impossibility of achieving work-life balance. Implicit in their response was the belief that *something* must give, either career or personal life. In her own view, as I see it, she had made a choice aligned with *all* her values.

Slaughter believes that having more women in leadership positions will help improve well-being for women, as will the increased ability to work from home (something the pandemic has clearly accelerated). As she puts it, 'Only when women wield power in sufficient numbers will we create a society that genuinely works for all women. That will be a society that works for everyone.'

As I've witnessed among younger people I mentor, many women and men are pushing for more flexible work schedules and better jobs — and succeeding in these efforts. One example is a woman named Piruze.

Negotiating for what you need

Piruze grew up in Turkey, studied in the US, and built an impressive, international career as a start-up founder, consultant and then as a division leader. In her early thirties, she was living in Singapore and building the Southeast Asia business for a fintech company.

Piruze spent more than five years at this fast-paced company, having gone from being the first person on the ground in the region, to being in an office with 150 people. She decided to take a sabbatical to focus on learning, pushing herself in areas she couldn't find the time to explore between a demanding job and a family. It might have seemed like a risky move, but she was confident she could do it and get back in again. During her sabbatical, she got pregnant, and then started looking for a new job.

She got a terrific offer to join a venture capital firm as a partner. This offer came while she was 12-weeks pregnant with her second child. The fact that her would-be new boss wanted to hire her, knowing full well that she'd be up for four months of maternity leave soon, speaks to the real changes happening at some firms in terms of valuing good employees and working to accommodate their whole lives.

As she was preparing to head back after maternity leave, she gave a lot of thought to how she could do an excellent job and still have enough time with her newborn. She decided to ask for a four-day work week as she started back. She presented it as a trial, to see if it would work, and brought in data.

> *I didn't just say, 'I want this and I want that'. I said, 'Hey, I talked to some people that I look up to, who were in my situation. This is the best practice that the best firms are doing now. I am looking forward to jumping back in to do my best in this job. Here are the steps.'*[4]

Her boss agreed to give it a try.

Not all firms are this flexible, as Piruze well knew. She picked this firm in part because she knew it had an open enough culture to consider her request.

> *Because of what I learned from my first mat leave, I wanted to make sure I was in an environment where I'd have enough flexibility and freedom to do the right thing for my job, but not put in extra hours just for the sake of it. I don't want to compromise on being ambitious, or getting results and growing the company, but I want to be careful to spend my time only on important things when I know there are going to be a lot of extra demands on my time.*

For Piruze, finding ways to succeed according to her terms in all areas of her life is part of helping change the landscape of work for women.

> *I feel like the previous generation had many more obstacles to overcome and had to choose either family or work,*

(continued)

because that was the world at the time. If this generation doesn't push the boundaries in the right way, the people we are giving birth to are going to look back at us and say, 'Why did you not at least try to be the change and make it an easier decision to have kids and have a career?' I really wanted to do something I would be proud of when returning from maternity leave. I think bringing in these flexibilities to work not only allows more people to put in their best, but also helps them to fully commit to their work, clients and mission, as they feel less guilty about the choices that they make in their personal lives.

I would even go so far as to say that work can help you achieve personal aims. Obviously we work to earn a living, relying on our careers to take care of our need for financial security, but our careers can also be the vehicle for other ambitions, such as moving overseas, making new friends and developing new skills or competencies.

Or, getting out a hammer and saw to remodel your Victorian house, a favourite pastime of Paul Bonk, a native Canadian who now lives in New York State. After driving a cab and doing manual labour jobs, Paul earned his PhD in political science from Rutgers University in New Jersey. He secured a tenure track position at a small teaching college in New York about 25 years ago, and has been there ever since.

Paul is married, raising a daughter, and utilising his carpentry skills by working on the Victorian house they live in. For Paul, whose favourite class to teach is sociology, every year at the college brings something new because the issues confronting society change. His job also allows him to focus on his family and his home, which are his other passions.

There are limits to using your job to achieve other aims. In theory, I suppose, I could have relied on my career to help me stay fit by becoming a lumberjack after all, or made myself read more books by working as a librarian. But in addition to being totally unqualified for a job requiring slinging an axe, I knew that no-one should take a job *strictly* for the added benefits. Most of your time at work will be spent doing your work; you have to enjoy it. Still, thinking about how your job might support your other aims is a good exercise to help break the habit of seeing these domains as always in competition.

Power Perspective #1: Embrace outside interests—and know they can contribute to career success

When I was 21 and just starting out in my career, I moved to New York City for my very first job at a bank. Once there, I started looking for a place to go swimming. I needed at least a 25-yard pool to do laps, my go-to exercise since my years on the junior high school swim team (and a short period of near-glory as a synchronised swimmer). Now, working in my first real job, I really needed that daily release.

Swimming pools were not a common feature in Manhattan's dense, built-up, glass-and-concrete urban landscape. The only pools I found were at the Downtown Athletic Club, which had a quota on people under the age of 25, and the New York Health and Racquet Club, which had many branches, primarily devoted to aerobics. The pools at the latter were the size of a large coffee mug, built so you could show off your body in a bathing suit after all those hours of jumping around.

I knew of one other pool in Lower Manhattan, close to my apartment in Greenwich Village: a brand new one at New York University. The university had just built a huge gym with a great swimming facility, a block-and-a-half from my place. But there was a catch: you had to be an NYU student to use the pool.

So there I was: a swimmer with no place to swim.

And then I got an idea: *I'll take a class at NYU! Why not?* If I took just one class, I could use the pool every single day. Going to school seemed like a small price to pay for a pool. It's always good to learn new things. And my bank employer would cover the cost of my education, as long as I earned a B or better. It would be like a free gym, with homework attached.

I had considered getting a graduate degree at some point in the future, maybe an MBA, perhaps at Stanford, where I grew up. But now I was in New York, near a good graduate program that included pool access. I thought: *Why not take a couple of classes in business and then maybe use those credits to transfer to Stanford later?*

I applied for the part-time MBA program at NYU. I got accepted, enrolled in two classes and joined the pool. The commute to the downtown campus for class was inconvenient, but I liked the educational content. The pool around the corner from my apartment was fabulous. It was love at first sight.

I went swimming every single day that semester. I also went on to complete my entire MBA at NYU. It took me four years, since I was working full time. This meant four years of daily swimming.

Having that MBA wound up being a great asset, one that helped me move into my next role and assume leadership positions early in my career. I would not have pursued an MBA right after college if not for my need to go swimming.

Our passions matter. Rather than detracting from a career, they can help support it, often in surprising ways. While some people try to ignore or minimise their personal desires in order to focus on their careers, our non-work passions are part of who we are. Embracing the various aspects of ourselves helps us thrive, creating energy and a sense of agency, both of which can empower us at work. Making room for non-work-related interests helps us get where we want to go – and love all parts of our lives. Your work and your passions are on the same team.

Our passions matter. Rather than detracting from a career, they can help support it, often in surprising ways.

Outside interests also support our careers over the long haul because they build our 'mental toolkit', says Art Markman, a professor of psychology and marketing at the University of Texas at Austin, and the author of a handful of books on thinking and success, including *Bring Your Brain to Work*. Markman says:

> ***Most of us don't realize how much the variety of experiences we have in our lives benefits the overall base of knowledge that we can draw on to be a success at work. We're not trained this way in education. All of our classes have names: English Class; Math Class. We're taught early on to segment our knowledge, to solve problems on math tests only with math solutions. We bring that approach to work. But actually, anything you know is fair game to solve a work problem.***[5]

Creative passions, in particular, can improve our ability to see things from different perspectives; this includes things like watercolour painting, bonsai gardening and writing poetry. As Markman says:

> ***When you do anything creative, you are forced to look at the world around you and see it from different perspectives. The research suggests that this can become a mindset, and it can be great at work.***

Seeing a situation from more than one perspective might help you access needed resources from a distracted or uncooperative colleague; for example, as Markman notes:

> ***Often, we try to convince someone to see things our way in order to get the resources we need. The alternative is to see it through their perspective and show them how supporting your project will make life better for them. If you legitimately understand what they're trying to accomplish and show them how what you're trying to do will help, that makes it a lot easier to get things done.***

Perspective-taking also could mean stopping to consider what might be bothering a colleague who is being difficult, and offering to help, rather than getting offended.

Power Perspective #2: Make work fun

My entry-level bank job kicked off with a six-month, intensive training program. There was a big group of us, all recent grads in our early twenties, and we all had to sit in these training classes for eight hours a day, week after week. The workday could feel very long and very tedious.

A fellow trainee named Jim got in the habit of starting the morning with *The New York Times* crossword puzzle. Inspired by his routine, the rest of us turned it into a group ritual. We started arriving early for this activity, stopping at a sidewalk cart on the way in to grab coffee and a donut (or a bran muffin, in my case). Then we'd all crowd around someone's desk, throwing out answers. It was fun and collaborative, and gave us energy for the day.

Fun matters. A fun, challenging group activity like the crossword puzzle can help people lighten up, express more of themselves and bring more enthusiasm to their actual work.

Helping employees have fun together can benefit the bottom line.

You can't expect your job to be 100 per cent enjoyable all the time, of course. It's *work*, generally defined as the exertion of mental or physical energy. Things that are relaxing and easy, like watching Netflix, usually do not include a salary. But while work can be taxing, it shouldn't feel like an unrelenting grind. Work is part of your life, and a *big* part; most people spend more hours working than doing any other single activity. Finding fun at work is a way to build the connection between your work life and your personal life, and to thrive in each domain.

For leaders, helping employees have fun together can benefit the bottom line. Fun helps people build real relationships, a key to productivity in many of today's collaborative work environments and industries. Employees are also likely to spend more time in the office if they're having fun, and to stay with the company longer. Having fun even leads to more creativity.

For all these reasons, many of today's top companies have campus-like environments to improve the experience of being at work. Twitter San Francisco has a rooftop garden with a corn hole game set. Microsoft has beach volleyball and electric cars. DropBox offers amazing chefs and meals, with beer and wine, and encourages people to hang out over dinner with colleagues, and even to bring their families. At Google, in addition to getting significant benefits such as paid parental leave, employees at campuses around the globe can play ping pong and video games, listen to jukeboxes, and use whimsical office upgrades, such as a slide in San Francisco and an indoor basketball court in Zürich. Employees in some offices can get in-house massages, work out in a rock-climbing gym and grab free lunch from high-end caterers.[6]

At one of the early Google campuses in California, there were a few 'conference bikes', bright yellow or red bicycles built for seven, ostensibly designed for holding meetings while getting some fresh air. Everyone would grab a seat and start pedalling. The seats faced inward, allowing cyclists to theoretically discuss important issues while pumping their legs. If everyone pedalled, the bike moved. It was not actually conducive to a focused discussion, but it was novel and silly and fun, making it a great way to take a break with co-workers and let down your guard.

While tech firms are known for creating fun offices, plenty of other companies have also adopted this approach. Patagonia has bikes, volleyball courts and yoga classes on-site.[7] PetSmart, Purina, Amazon, Ben & Jerry's and Bissel allow employees to bring their dogs to work. Studies show that a furry friend can ease social interactions and reduce stress.[8] In our post-pandemic world, with more employees wanting to work from home, companies will likely invest energy in making office spaces appealing – and functional for the collaborative work that's harder to do when working from home. They will also likely invest in ways to have fun together remotely.

Whether or not your company offers games or gardens, you can increase your enjoyment of your job on your own. One way is to develop friendships at work. This often happens naturally; at the bank, a group of us who were new to New York and single would regularly go out to lunch or dinner together. Even if your office isn't particularly social, chances are there's at least one person you like there. Make the effort to foster a friendship.

In fields where collaboration is a key to success, some people see socialising as part of getting the job done. When Wendy Paris, my co-writer on this book, was working as a production assistant at the PBS station in Houston, one of her first jobs in a long string of journalism jobs, she was struck by the efforts the crew made to connect socially. Wendy says:

> ***Before a big shoot, the videographers would go out for beer and Star pizza, a Houston favourite. The next day on the set, they'd have all these inside jokes from the night before. The videographer I worked with the most often, a hugely talented guy, talked about how joking around over pizza helped him be creative the next day, and remember that this was a fun job and not 'brain surgery'. It lowered the stress level about trying to do everything just right and let everyone be more focused in the moment.***

The pandemic may have made it easier to break down barriers that inhibit connection in certain cases. 'When you're remote, you do need to have relationships with people [and] that in itself has forced people to open up a bit', says Perth-based career coach Helen Holan.[9] Seeing a co-worker's living room (or closet) on Zoom, and sharing your own, can create a sense of intimacy and remind you of your common humanity. You may be able to build on this peek into another person's life to help deepen a budding friendship.

Some people specifically choose jobs that offer a promising social life. If you're hoping that work will help you make friends, consider applying to large companies that often need to do big hires all at once, such as Salesforce, IBM, or big legal and financial services firms. This guarantees that there will be other newcomers around, also looking to connect. You can even ask about the social environment during an interview, though as my recent-grad son, Zachary, and his friends have discovered, companies with large intakes of young people will often tell you about that fact early on, no questions needed.

Many people make lasting friendships at work, especially in the beginning of a career. Young people often work long hours together, have free time after work and haven't yet formed numerous (sometimes demanding) adult social relationships. A lot of the people I met at my bank training program are still good friends, including one of my best friends. Many other people from that job have also stayed close.

Even smaller offices can lead to close, lasting connections. This may be especially true if you go to an overseas branch of a large firm and find yourself leaning on, and really valuing, the presence of your peers, something Emily Huo discovered when she moved to Singapore in her twenties.

Bonding over being overseas

Emily Huo transferred from San Francisco to Singapore in 2013 to work at Twitter. It was her first time moving to another country for a full-time job. She was excited about the opportunity and the adventure.

Adjusting to life on this island nation definitely took time. Her new friendships at work really helped. The other young, single people at work quickly became her support system, helping her feel more rooted.

> ***There were a lot of us who had transitioned in the same capacity: women, around the same age, in the same boat, from the US, London, Dublin. We transplants would grab dinner after work, because if we didn't, we'd be cooking for ourselves alone, which is actually more expensive than eating out in Singapore. We'd also travel together on weekends, hop on a one-hour flight to Bali, or take a ferry to Indonesia. Anyone between around 23 and 35 who wasn't married, including folks at Twitter Singapore who were locals or had gone to school there, kind of fell into this social circle.***[10]

For Emily, this circle of work friends quickly became a major part of the joy of the job. Then, when Lisa Wang, another young Chinese-American woman from San Francisco, moved to Singapore by herself, Emily made it her mission to pay that help forward by befriending her.

> ***I'd gone through that exact same process of moving and not knowing anyone. I'd tell her things like, 'These are the areas you want to live in for your first year. Don't go further than these subway stations. Don't live more than 10 minutes' walk, tops, from an MRT station, because of that heat', even though in San Francisco, we were used to walking a lot.***

(continued)

These friendships have also lasted. After three years in Singapore, Emily transferred back to San Francisco. She says that while she's certainly made friends at work in the States, the intensity isn't the same.

> *The friendships from Singapore are at a different level. When you travel with people, you know them so much better. It's been more than five years since I left, and we're spread out across the world, but we stay in touch all the time.*

As Emily saw, work can generate friendships that may well last for life. Sometimes, stepping further outside of your comfort zone for a job can help you bring people closer.

Power Perspective #3: There are very few truly 'wrong' decisions (so don't agonise over them)

Do I take this offer and start right away? Or do I wait to see if something better comes along?

I want to live abroad, but will moving mean missing out on opportunities at home?

Should I stop just following my work interests wherever they lead, and be more intentional about my path?

These kinds of questions can plague job-seekers, and even those well into their careers. It can feel scary to make a decision, partly because a choice for one thing is a choice away from something else; no one wants to miss the best opportunity. How do you weigh the value of stability versus adventure or of a small salary at a cool start-up versus a larger one at a less interesting firm?

Most of us have faced some similar quandary. We may assume we can figure out the best path if we just think about it hard enough. We make 'pros and cons' lists. We analyse and agonise. We worry. Meanwhile, we don't make a decision.

Endless questioning gives every choice too much power, suggesting that you can only thrive if every single aspect of your life falls into place (which it rarely does). Indecision can also morph into a habit of second-guessing decisions once you've made them, and of spending too much time in doubt and worry. Fearing that you might 'miss out' on something better is a kind of scarcity mentality, a way of perceiving the world of work as limited and small.

Endless questioning gives every choice too much power.

This decision-making paralysis is common, and it is increased by the feeling that your work and your life are on opposite teams. In truth, though, there is rarely one 'wrong' choice that will limit your options forever. Recognising this fact can make it easier to decide.

At the beginning of a career, a job at any good firm will teach you something. You may be choosing between a non-profit and a corporate position, or the private sector and government. Any of these options can be a good start, and not much precludes switching later. The same is true if you're considering joining a large, established firm or a small start-up. For the first 10 years of most careers, at least, you can try different things without worrying about shutting down options. As you get older, the jobs you've taken funnel you into a stream of sorts, as do your skills and knowledge – but the 'stream' can be quite wide. My switch to Google at age 47 came after having never worked in tech.

In the tech industry, the product imperative is 'test and iterate'. This approach can apply to jobs, too. Give it some thought, but then, make a choice. Throw yourself into it. Then tweak as needed. People change jobs every two or three years now, and it's perfectly acceptable.

Whatever your age or stage, the only real way to know the outcome of a decision is to make one, throw yourself into it and see what happens. You really can't suss out the future through endless thinking, and it's far better to make a choice and commit to it than to sap your energy trying. Commitment builds energy, which helps you do your job well and succeed.

Committing to a job creates forward momentum, as Emily Rubin saw once she finally decided to accept her first real offer and begin her career.

The value of making a choice

I met Emily Rubin, 22, through my son Zachary. They'd both gone to Emory University, and following graduation, Emily entered a COVID-hit world, and was struggling to land her first real job.

After months of looking, Emily got an offer for an entry-level position at a San Francisco–based software company. She'd be working on a platform connecting employers needing text and document annotation to gig workers. Emily was relieved – and ambivalent. She just wasn't sure she should take it. The starting salary was so low that she worried about surviving on it in San Francisco. Should she keep looking for something better? What if she got to San Francisco and couldn't cover her living expenses? What would happen then? She'd been on the job hunt for a while, but could there still be something better out there?

I suggested she try asking for a higher starting salary, and then make a choice.

She agreed to try, and was told that they don't negotiate for entry-level salaries. Emily really wanted to start working somewhere, and was excited about every other part of the offer. I suggested she just take it and give it a try. While the salary wasn't ideal, she could make it work, and it's always easier to get a job when you have a job. If it didn't work out, she'd be well placed to find something better.

Emily took the job. 'I realized that I wasn't going to die out there in San Francisco on this low salary. I actually am a responsible person', she says. She moved to San Francisco and threw herself into her work.[11]

Flash forward nine months: she'd grown to hate the job due to management issues at the company – not the salary. She was unhappy enough that I agreed she should leave, even though she hadn't stayed a year or two, which is usually the amount of time needed to really learn something and grow in a position. She looked for another role and found a position at Huron Consulting Group, then quit the start-up. She didn't take the original job in order to move across the country and land a new, better role. But choosing something and really going for it allowed her to gain work experience, learn to love a new city and build a foundation for her next role.

In my own case, after about five years of working at the bank, I'd finished my MBA and my freestyle looked great (and my apartment smelled like chlorine). I began to be curious about other careers. I was doing well, and had been promoted, but I wanted to know what else was out there. I'd focused on marketing in my MBA and was interested in exploring that field.

American Express was recruiting MBA grads at NYU, and I got offered a job in marketing there. It was still in financial services, my background to date, so it was an easier transition than if I'd tried to switch roles and industries simultaneously. I went to work for an inspiring manager, a woman who had also gotten her MBA from NYU and seemed like a great boss and one who would be interested in helping me develop in my career. I was excited to go work for her.

She *was* a terrific boss. But then she left within three months of my arrival. I had a new manager, which changed the experience completely. I felt the new boss was not focused on helping me develop and I found her unpleasant to be around. I hadn't been at the company long enough to develop any advocates, and I had no one to go to for help within the firm. (See chapter 3 to learn about the importance of creating sponsors at work.)

I was really distressed. Since it was only my second job, I was terrified that if I quit, people would think ill of me, assuming my short stay indicated something was wrong with me. But I knew I couldn't stay. I started thinking about what I wanted to do next.

I had always wanted to live overseas, but I had limited language skills (as in, I only spoke English, despite studying French in middle and high school.) In college, I'd had the opportunity to spend six months in England, a half-year abroad that met my language needs and convinced me that I didn't need to return: water-logged air, soggy vegetables. The movie *Crocodile Dundee* had recently come out, which made everything about Australia seem fun and exotic. Australians spoke English, and the continent was close to Asia, a region I'd long been interested in.

A friend suggested I look for a job as a consultant, since I now had finance and marketing experience. I knew nothing about the industry but started looking into consulting jobs in Australia and found one. I took the role and moved to Sydney for it.

I loved Australia and the job. When the firm I was working for became part of BCG, I stayed on, living in Australia for nine years. I then transferred with BCG to Singapore, where I lived for another four years. During that 13-year stint, I got married (to my Aussie husband Linton) and we had our two sons. In 1999, we all moved back to the US because I'd been offered an exciting new role to build the international division at the American multinational financial services company Charles Schwab.

Similar to Emily's case, a decision that ultimately did not work out (taking the job at Amex) helped push me toward a new adventure and a series of interesting jobs.

While it's easy to worry that one wrong move will set your life off on a misguided course forever, in fact, careers are very long. You can always correct the course, turn around and try again. There are very few 'one way doors'. And even bad moves can lead you to good ones.

Power Perspective #4: See the serendipity in your life ... and act on it

If you look back at the high points in your life, how many came from a serendipitous encounter, something you hadn't planned? If you're like me, probably a lot of them. Noticing the serendipity around you and *acting on it* can lead to amazing experiences in your personal life – and sometimes to career opportunities you never imagined. Seizing the serendipity is an important part of remembering that your work and your personal life are on the same team, and being open to how it all unfolds.

I love the story of the artist MC Escher taking a cruise one winter to escape the snow in Switzerland where he was living at the time.[12] While touring buildings in Spain, he found himself entranced by the geometrical Moorish designs, specifically how the motif repeated itself 'according to a certain system.' This was what he wanted to do too, he realised, but with animals or objects rather than with abstract shapes. This vision contributed to the development of his distinctive approach to image-making and his success as one of the most innovative artist-mathematicians of all time. He didn't take the cruise to generate great new ideas for his work; he set out for the sea *to escape the snow*. But that led him to have a serendipitous encounter with Moorish design, which he responded to back in his studio. It's an amazing example of the power of serendipity.

Leveraging serendipity for your career can take work. After that trip to Spain, MC Escher returned to his studio and worked tirelessly on his drawings, striving to figure out how to incorporate this new insight. Serendipity does not replace hard work and education, planning and preparation, feedback and communication. Nor is it the same thing as 'dumb luck'. I'm always encouraging people I mentor not to explain away their success as luck, particularly women. If you talk about a great new job by saying, 'Oh, I was lucky', you may think you're being humble, but in fact, you're diminishing the role of your own actions in generating your outcomes. You're minimising your agency. Success requires owning your efforts. But serendipity can be the thing that takes all your work and spins it off in a new, exciting direction.

I think of serendipity as an equation: Opportunity + Action = Serendipity.

Opportunity + Action = Serendipity

Seeing the serendipity and acting on it also requires maintaining an open mind about your path. Psychologist Art Markman cautions people against what he calls, 'editing life in a forward direction', basically shutting out or ignoring opportunities that don't match a predetermined script of what you imagined for yourself. Markman says:

> ***The world is more interesting than our imaginations. If we cut out anything that doesn't conform to what we believed our lives would be about, we miss out on a lot of opportunities that are way more interesting than what we thought would happen.***[13]

In my own life, my switch from financial services to tech was sparked by a serendipitous encounter. In 2006, I was still living in San Francisco, after having moved there with Charles Schwab. That job had ended (see chapter 2) and I'd moved to Visa International, where I was running the company's commercial card product globally.

I had a good job. But all the energy and excitement in the Bay Area was around the Internet. It seemed like everyone was talking about tech. I felt like I was missing something interesting. The first dot.com bubble was long past, and companies building businesses based around the Internet were on the rise. Why wasn't I involved?

Around this time, Visa decided to pursue a partnership with Google. A team of us had a small meeting with Vint Cerf, a Google evangelist – and one of the people who designed the Internet. After that exploratory meeting, it fell to me to follow up. I sent Vint a thank you note through my work account. Then, since I now had Vint Cerf's email, I sent a second, more personal, email from my private account. I shared the fact that I was a bit bored in my career in financial services and was curious to learn more about what was happening in the digital arena. I asked him if he thought anyone at Google would talk to me and/or ever consider hiring someone with my background.

It was a little nervy to ask about a possible job through a connection made at my current job, but it wasn't an outrageous move to make. You are always allowed to look for a better job, even if your current employer is fair and you're doing well. You have to be discreet about looking for a new position, especially if doing so could upset your current employer. But cautious audacity is often rewarded.

Vint Cerf wrote back, asking me to send a résumé.

He circulated my résumé within Google, and I had a variety of discussions and interviews with different people at the company. About a year after I sent that first email to Vint, I joined Google to drive online ad sales and operations in APAC. This position would mean moving back to Singapore, which my husband and I were both excited to do. That job shaped the entire second half of my career, and had a huge impact on my family life.

If I hadn't followed up on that serendipitous encounter with Vint Cerf via email, I don't know if I would have gone into tech, at least not at that time and in that way. Would I be living in Singapore and Australia today? I don't know. But I do know that by seizing the serendipity of being placed in a small room with a global tech leader, I was able to move into an exciting new field that intrigued me, and that has helped me rise and thrive.

Serendipity can be useful even if following it leads to a dead end. A young American living in Australia who I know recently had a fluky opportunity to audition for a reality TV show shooting in Sydney. The producers were seeking someone with a 'real' American accent. He's not an actor and he had a job at the time, but the chance came up, so he took it.

He got the role. And he quickly discovered that he hated reality TV, and disliked the entire field of television production. To me, this is another great example of the power of serendipity. This young man was open to a career change, and commercial TV production accounts for about $334 million in Australia, annually.[14] This (negative) experience was useful because it quenched any burgeoning desire he might have had for a career in TV. It was also fun for a while and introduced him to a slew of new people who may well circle back into his life in some beneficial way in the future.

One small action, one big opportunity

Sandra Barron is an American writer and communications associate with the calm, focused energy of someone who does a lot of yoga. She had been living in Tokyo for seven years with her

(*continued*)

then-boyfriend/now-husband, working as a freelance journalist and enjoying the chance to get to know a new country. In 2014, they decided to move back to the US to be near her husband's father in Los Angeles. Through a serendipitous conversation with someone she knew in Japan, Sandra landed a full-time position as an LA-based associate producer for Japan's national television network, NHK. She was thrilled to find a journalism job in LA, and one that would allow her to use her Japanese.

After a few years in the position, however, she grew frustrated with the low pay and lack of opportunities for advancement. She started looking for another journalism job in Los Angeles, but kept hitting dead ends. One night, while scrolling through her Facebook feed, she happened to see a post from a British guy she'd known in Tokyo. He had started a travel agency, and posted that he needed a coordinator to help arrange high-end boutique trips to Japan, someone who really knew the country. 'It sounded like a dream job', Sandra says, 'but I could not move back to Japan'.[15]

Still, she sent the guy a note on Facebook, saying how great the company sounded, and that it was too bad he wasn't seeking a remote employee.

Well ... maybe he was, he wrote back. His team had been struggling to navigate the time zone difference between Tokyo and their New York-based tour partners. A person on the West Coast might be ideal, he said. He hadn't advertised for one because it had just seemed like an impossible find. 'He said I sounded perfect', Sandra says.

They began corresponding by email, then met in person in Japan to discuss the details of how it might work. Because of that serendipitous Facebook post – and the actions they both took in response – in 2018, Sandra quit NHK and took a much-desired, valuable role at the travel agency.

Flash forward to 2019, before the pandemic. Sandra had been working remotely for the Japanese-based boutique travel agency and enjoying it. But when the team took office space in Tokyo, she became the only remote employee in a company that relied on constant communication. Being in LA had proven a little trickier than anticipated all along, but now it began to feel impossible. Soon, Sandra was retrenched. 'I could tell things weren't really working out, but I hadn't expected it to end so suddenly', she says. 'I had never been let go before. I was reeling emotionally, and not sure where to find another job.'

Meanwhile, she had an interview lined up to lead bike tours by the beach on weekends, just for fun. Now she had free time during the work week, too. 'I went in to the interview and said, "Initially, I was just available to do tours on the weekends, but now it looks like I'm available all week too!"'

She started leading tours along the beach, and when the company asked her to help out at the bike shop with rentals and sales, she agreed.

She soon found herself cycling 3 miles to the shop at sunrise, standing on her feet all day, hauling bikes off shelves, and leading 8-mile bike tours, sometimes twice a day.

> ***I went from sitting at my desk all the time to riding my bike sometimes 20 miles a day. I lost 15 pounds, and I felt totally jacked. I got to use my Japanese and hear all these stories. It was fun and social and it gave me a huge amount of optimism and energy.***

She needed that energy for the job search, which, once again, was leading to a lot of dead ends. Her serendipitous bike shop job helped her stay on task, and she eventually got a full-time, remote position doing enterprise copywriting for Microsoft. 'All that biking and talking to people at the shop kept me from getting discouraged when things didn't come through', she says.

After starting in her new role at Microsoft, she continued working at the bike shop and leading tours on Saturdays. When she and her husband moved inland to be closer to his job, the commute

(*continued*)

to the beach was too long to be practical, so she gave up her bike shop gig. Today, thinking about her former part-time job gives her a broader perspective on work.

> *On bad days at work, sometimes I'll think: at the bike shop, I could just fix a flat tire and ring up a line of people instead of dealing with the sixth round of revisions. It's not like it's a real option, but it reminds me that I have a certain amount of resilience. I will get through, no matter what.*

We've all heard stories of serendipitous encounters that led to amazing opportunities. (Or even to romance; I've heard of more than one couple who met on a flight or at the grocery store.) Someone attends a party and meets someone who offers them a dream job. An aspiring actor goes to lunch at a new place and is spotted by an agent who lands them a leading role. These stories are always exciting, and they do happen; sometimes that kind of major serendipity occurs. More often, however, the transformational moments in our lives are smaller and arrive with less of a bang. Our effort to follow up on an unexpected introduction or respond to something that piques our interest is what adds up to real value.

Seize the serendipity 101

Opportunity may knock on the door at your office, as in my case with Vint Cerf, or show up on your Facebook feed. But other times, it's not as obvious. Here's how to notice the serendipity and take action.

- **Be open.** Potential hovers around us. Make a habit of looking for unexpected opportunities. Really listen to the people you meet and the conversations you have; what do they know that might be of interest to you? Getting to know others can lead to amazing connections and opportunities.
- **Follow up.** Often, making serendipity work for you is all about the follow-up. If you hear a great talk or meet a person whose

career path intrigues you, follow up with an email expressing your appreciation and your interest in an informational interview. You don't need to have a specific goal in mind or a formal introduction.

- **Make the ask.** If you have a specific request, as I did with Vint Cerf, go ahead and make it. It may feel brazen, but what seems audacious to you is often not such a big deal to the other person.
- **Respond to requests.** As you progress in your career, people will take inspiration from you and reach out for advice. Have a quick conversation with those who ask, and answer their emails. You may worry that you won't be able to help, but often merely sharing something you've learned – or reassuring them that their experience is 'normal' – is exactly what they need to hear.

Takeaways

- Your personal and professional life are on the same team. Move past the old mindset of 'my work OR my life.' Find synergies between them.
- Embrace your passions outside of work. Personal interests enliven you (and may help with your career in surprising ways).
- Have fun! Enjoying yourself at work supports camaraderie, commitment and creativity.
- Don't obsess about making the right choice. There is no 'one wrong' decision' that will derail your career dreams. There are many routes to a fulfilling, successful life.
- Commit to a decision long enough to gain from it. Then, if it isn't where you want to be, 'iterate' – as in, make a change and *move on*.
- Opportunity + Action = Serendipity. Look for serendipity around you, and act on it.

mindshift two

Stamina is a muscle. Build yours!

Power perspectives in this chapter

- make time for self-care
- don't over-focus on the negative
- remember that you have options
- acknowledge that you are not totally in control.

I met a young woman, who I'll call Barbara, on a business trip to California. She was working at a successful new company, at the start of her career and proud of her position as her company's first ever sales manager. It's exciting to hold the 'first' job within an organisation. You help set the tone and scope of the position. Also, the company was beginning to take off and, suddenly, even her own family and friends were talking about it. For a young person early in her career, she was ideally placed.

But Barbara had just been hit with what felt like very bad news. She was going to be 'layered over'. The company was hiring a new person above her to run North American sales. He'd be inserted between her and her current boss, so that now, instead of heading sales herself, she'd be an employee in the department she had created.

This change felt like a huge blow. She worried that it would decrease her status and authority. Her salary wasn't changing, but her enthusiasm about her job and her abilities definitely waned. She also told me that she was afraid she was 'getting old' and running out of chances to rise. (At twenty-something? Old? By her standard, I should have been retired, perfecting my golf swing and dining at 5 pm.) She reached out for advice. Should she quit?

I didn't think she should quit. Having a person inserted above you can feel like a demotion, for sure, but within a high-growth company, it often isn't. It certainly wasn't in her case. She was doing very well at her job, but the company was growing exponentially. The company needed someone with deeper experience. Barbara was still pretty inexperienced and young (despite her worries about her age). She didn't have the background that the company thought was needed for this senior role.

Also, I happened to know the new hire, and I thought he was a great leader and someone who cared about developing his people. I believed Barbara would learn a lot from working for him. I encouraged her to stick it out, and to work on developing more *stamina* for the vagaries of work (rather than working on her résumé and seeking a new job).

She decided to stay put and give it a try. She very quickly adjusted to the new boss and began to thrive again. The experience of succeeding at her job created more energy for work, which translated into more success. She wound up landing one promotion then another from her new boss. She even got promoted *while out on maternity leave*, which shouldn't be a shocking detail, but sadly still is in some corporations. She was there for another four-plus years, and has since moved on and continued to rise.

The 'Ah-ha!' of Barbara's story: stamina is a success superpower

When people leave perfectly good jobs or stay far too long in bad ones, it's easy to blame poor decision-making or bad luck or a lack of self-discipline. But often, as I've seen, the real problem is inadequate stamina. You need stamina to stick with a job after being layered over, for example, as in Barbara's case. Your feelings are hurt. You don't know how it will pan out. You have to hang in there when disappointed, rather than quitting prematurely or stewing with resentment, and letting that decrease your productivity and enthusiasm.

You also need stamina to look for a better job when it's time to move on or you've been let go. Stamina helps you pursue better opportunities at your current place of work, and stick in there without losing hope. It takes stamina to move to a new city or country and create new contacts and friends. Or if you're leading a team and must continually advocate for them to get the resources they need to do their jobs. Or to fight back when you have been wronged. These are all typical examples of the role of stamina at work. We tend to think about stamina in terms of athletics, but it is also a key characteristic of those who have rewarding, *long* careers.

Some people face extremely challenging political, economic and/or personal factors and have to call on reserves of stamina that most of us will never need to tap. I mentor a young Afghan woman who had gone to university in Bangladesh, but was back home in Kabul when the country fell to the Taliban in 2021. Talking to her on WhatsApp as the Taliban surrounded the city, and then losing all contact when the city fell, definitely made my own 'challenges' with stamina seem miniscule and insignificant.

She did eventually get out to safety, I'm happy to report. But the ongoing challenges she has surmounted in her effort to build a stable life certainly put in perspective the kinds of struggles most of us face. Thinking about her situation also points to another aspect of stamina: when we hear stories of people who miraculously rose above incredibly difficult circumstances, you can bet that stamina played a part.

We often talk about stamina as 'just doing it' or 'gritting it out'. But this is not what I mean. Forcing yourself to stick with tasks you hate can lead to burnout and to giving up. Repeatedly saying to yourself, 'Just do it!' and 'Stop complaining!' saps energy, rather than generating it.

I think of career stamina as something far more positive. It's that initial discipline or perseverance *plus* the positive force of enthusiasm. Enthusiasm grows from liking what you're doing and succeeding at it.

Stamina is a virtuous cycle. Working hard with enthusiasm generally leads to accomplishment and success. That experience of success in turn helps generate more enthusiasm and energy, which leads to more wins. I see stamina as an empowerment equation: Perseverance + Enthusiasm = Stamina.

Perseverance + Enthusiasm = Stamina.

Stamina helps create a sense of agency in your life. And unlike an immutable, personal characteristic you're born with, such as having blue eyes, say, stamina can be built. You develop career stamina much as a runner builds stamina for a big race – by practising specific skills and mental habits, and avoiding others. Part of loving your day job is incorporating regular stamina 'mental workouts' into your normal routine. Here's how.

Power Perspective #1: Self-care supports stamina

If you work in healthcare, self-care is part of the job description. In all professions, it's an important part of building and maintaining career stamina. As Ralph Waldo Emerson put it, 'The first wealth is health'.

The importance of self-care became obvious during the pandemic, when the lockdown put an end to most social outings and shuttered recreational outlets such as gyms, theatres and restaurants. Many people saw firsthand how the lack of these kinds of activities can lead to lethargy, burnout and emotional distress (such that not even weekly bread baking could alleviate). Even minor-seeming acts of self-care help us be at our personal best; when we're not, many normal activities can seem overwhelming.[1] This can include things like getting up to go to work, meeting clients and making decisions.

Even minor-seeming acts of self-care help us be at our personal best.

One of the most important forms of self-care can be done lying down (and should be): sleep. Inadequate sleep is associated with a slew of poor outcomes, including cognitive decline and psychological distress.

Arianna Huffington, who has written extensively on the importance of sleep and has referred to herself as an 'insomniac turned sleep evangelist', experienced first-hand the price of inadequate sleep when she collapsed from exhaustion. As she puts it, 'It's only relatively recently that we've come to fully grasp the medical consequences of sleep deprivation'.[2]

Sleep studies point to another important form of self-care, one that generally requires getting out of bed and getting dressed: social support. I always think about the spectators at marathons who stand on the sidelines and eagerly hand out bottles of water to the runners. Marathoners need hydration and a lot of stamina. Those cheering fans offering water also provide a stamina-boosting dose of social support. Social support is so important that, during the pandemic, some sports teams competed in empty stadiums filled with cardboard cut-outs of fans. Even paper people, it turns out, can help increase stamina.

I belong to three book clubs, not only because I like reading, but also because the members are part of my support team. I also count on my husband and friends for social support. Companies increasingly pay for career coaches for senior and mid-level managers, not only to help them improve their leadership skills, but also because this regular human support helps spark better performance.

Good self-care can also mean spending time alone: taking a walk in the woods, drawing, cooking, gardening or working out. I try to take a break every day to do something physical. An hour at the gym, doing laps in the pool or being out on the court playing badminton helps me to refocus and relieve tension. Many forms of self-care go together, like hiking and chatting with a friend, or my reading groups that let me escape into a novel and get out of my own thoughts, as well as socialise.

Self-care can be particularly important during moments of career upheaval. The support of friends and time spent doing personally nourishing activities can help you maintain the stamina you need to keep going, as a woman I'll call Colette recently realised.

Stamina to get back out there and try again

Colette is a serious-minded, super-social person in her mid-thirties who built a career in non-profit, social purpose work. She was doing well in a new role, but then, less than two years after she arrived, and right before the pandemic, the company reorganised and eliminated her position.

Poof! Her job was gone.

Colette had never lost a job in her life. 'Before this happened, the thought of losing my job felt like the worst thing that could happen in the world', she says. Being let go wasn't a result of her own performance, but it felt personal.

Colette reached out to friends for advice. Many people she knew had lost a job at some point in their careers, she discovered, people her own age and older, even successful friends much further along in their careers. 'It helped me recognise that this is normal, and that it's not a black mark on me. It doesn't mean that I'm not good at what I do', she says.

She started opening up about her experience while hiking with friends in the parks on the outskirts of her city.

> ***A friend and I would go on weekly walks. She'd been through a similar experience a year or two before. I feel like I hiked my way through my feelings. Moving my body was really important, and being able to talk to someone who'd had a similar experience at the same time really helped.***

Colette was out of work for six months, during which time she did some virtual interviews. She quickly realised that she needed to take control of how she internalised the interview experience to maintain her stamina in the face of rejections.

> ***In every interview conversation, I reminded myself that I wanted a job that was going to be a piece of my career and part of my purpose. I was interviewing them, too. I went***

> *into interviews looking to see if it was a good mutual fit. That approach really helped me avoid feeling like I was on the chopping block every time. If an interview didn't go well, instead of thinking, 'Wow, I really blew it!' I could step back and think, 'Wow, there wasn't good chemistry there'.*
>
> Colette landed an interview for a fundraising position at a non-profit she'd long admired.
>
> *We had a great conversation. It felt different from other interviews. When I described how my unique experiences connected with the job, I felt like the interviewer understood. That really made me feel like I would be a good fit.*
>
> She got the job and began working remotely during the pandemic, then moved cities and into the office when it reopened. 'It's absolutely where I want to be', she says.

Power Perspective #2: Don't over-focus on the negative

Disappointments and moments of discouragement will happen in your career; you can't prevent it. Organisations grow, shrink and pivot. They make structural changes frequently. These transformations have nothing to do with you. Though they are no reflection on your work or your worth, they can make you feel terrible. Other times, a setback *is* due to your performance. It's important to listen to feedback and adjust your behaviour accordingly. But even then, a rejection or failure generally won't determine how you do in the long run.

Your manner of dealing with it, however, does.

Obsessing about setbacks doesn't make them go away (even though rehashing all the gory details can feel very compelling, I know!). Negative rumination can, however, damage your career because it saps stamina. I've seen the tendency to fixate on the negative during performance reviews. If I tell people nine good things they've done, and offer one piece of constructive feedback, they'll focus all of their energy on that single critique. It's important to listen to constructive feedback in order to progress and thrive, sure, but you *also* have to really hear and think about the positive input during an assessment of your performance, something we will discuss later.

A rejection or failure generally won't determine how you do in the long run. Your manner of dealing with it, however, does.

We all focus on the negative to some degree. Rejection and criticism hurt, and we can't help thinking about these painful experiences. We examine decisions that led to undesirable outcomes as a way to avoid making the same mistake in the future. Dwelling on the negative is a natural tendency. Psychologists call this tendency a 'negativity bias', and the human species developed it for a purpose. 'People have evolved to pay more attention to negative information and experiences than to positive ones', says Glenn Geher, an evolutionary psychologist at the State University of New York at New Paltz. 'Negative information is threatening. Circumventing those threats in the future has a big payoff.'[3]

Unfortunately, when it comes to the kinds of disappointments and setbacks we face in the modern world, our negativity bias 'can bite us in the butt in a lot of ways', says Geher, 'such as by making us overly anxious'. Or by making us feel that we should obsess about every change or disappointment at work.

The better, more stamina-supporting approach to setbacks? Notice when our emotions have gotten the upper hand and then talk them back down, using facts and clear thinking. Psychologists call this 'reappraisal', and research shows that it can really help. 'You look at how you're appraising the situation, then see if you can reappraise it better', says Geher. Your immediate thought might be, *Someone else got the job I wanted. I must be terrible.* Geher says:

> ***A reappraisal could be, 'I didn't actually fit the job description perfectly.' Or, 'It's an over-flooded job market right now and there are a lot of other applicants.' That kind of reappraisal can really work. Not always, but it's usually one of the best tools we have.***

It's important to make a conscious effort to focus on your successes throughout your career because positive emotions help shore up stamina. Research bears out the power of positive emotions. Experiments inducing positive emotions have shown that they 'broaden the scope of visual attention', while fMRI studies (measuring brain activity) show that positive emotions literally expand people's field of vision. Barbara Fredrickson, a psychologist at the University of North Carolina at Chapel Hill, has devoted years to researching the value of positive emotions and experiences. Even small positive moments, such as witnessing a beautiful sunset or getting a bag of candy, can improve people's focus and performance at their jobs. (No wonder tech firms offer so many kinds of treats and snacks to workers for free.)

Positive moments build 'durable personal resources', such as creativity, energy, enthusiasm and drive. Psychologists see positive emotions as another part of our evolutionary toolkit. The purpose of positive emotions, as shaped over millions of years of evolution and natural selection, is to help build resources people need to survive.[4]

In other words, focusing on the positive helps you stay in the game.

As Fredrickson and others have shown, negative emotions, in contrast, can result in a narrowing of perception and more limited ideas. Finding yourself in a mental 'crouch' can shrink your range of vision and ability to generate solutions.

I often coach people on this skill when helping them prepare for job interviews. Young women, in particular, will talk about the qualifications they might be missing and the experiences they haven't had. They sometimes don't realise their strengths or know that companies don't expect as much from people early in their careers. I remind them to talk about what they *have* done. If asked about leadership experience, talk about when they worked as a camp counsellor or were part of student government. If asked about teamwork, mention their years on a sports team, the debate team, or the robotics club. If questioned about taking initiative, mention a club they started or events they organised. If asked about analytics, talk about their participation in the university's student investment management group. These experiences count and display real strengths.

Sharing your strengths helps hiring managers do their job. Most companies are looking for people with a couple of really strong areas, or 'spikes', as opposed to perfect all-arounders. Increasingly, companies focus on leveraging strengths, and you should, too. Yes, you need to improve areas of weaknesses, but (barring any major, career-destroying problems) it's far more important to identify your strengths and build on them. In an interview, emphasise your strong points and sketch for interviewers the connection between your experiences and what's needed for the position. You can always add the fact that you are curious to learn about other areas.

Another reason not to let a setback discourage you is that the opportunity you lost may well come back around. The first runner-up sometimes gets the crown. The reasons for this vary. The top candidate might withdraw. A new person might be put on the reviewing team. A background check might yield such high praise of you that the firm elevates you in the ranking. You don't know what's going to happen until the very end because recruiting isn't usually a transparent process, and many factors are at play.

A woman I know was the compromise candidate between two factions at a professional services firm. The partnership group was polarised. Each faction had a clear favourite, and neither would agree on the other's first choice. Since my friend was everyone's second choice, they decided to offer her the position.

She could have worried that everyone would know she wasn't the first pick or that this reflected on her ability or fit. But no one ever remembers the process. (Like all the kids who enter universities off the wait-list and go on to be excellent students and leaders, what counts is what you do when you get there.) She took the job, and threw herself into it. She's still there, getting good reviews and loving her work.

People often look at my career today, after I've been at it for 40 years, and assume my success has been constant and steady, with no disappointments along the way. As with most people who've had long and vibrant work lives, this is not true. I've lost out on desired jobs, then had them come back around.

After my brief, disappointing stint in marketing at American Express, when I was looking for a job as a consultant in Australia, I got pretty far along in the process with a small Sydney-based firm (from chapter 1). The lead partner there told me that, as a later applicant, I was number five out of four. If one of their first four dropped out, I could have the job. (He is a charming salesperson, but even he couldn't make that situation sound appealing.)

Being 'wait-listed' for a job I wanted didn't make me feel great. In the end, though, one of their offerees declined the position. I took the job and moved to Sydney. I did well and stayed there longer than any of the other three people hired in that round. No one remembered that I was fifth out of four.

Later, when I was eligible to be considered for partner at what had then become BCG, four of us were up at the same time, three men and me, the most senior woman in the office.

Two of the men made partner. The third did not. Nor did I. It's fairly common to not make partner at the first opportunity, but it was disappointing.

When I asked for feedback, one person told me I was too informal with my clients, as evidenced by the fact that they were kissing me hello. Clients often would kiss me on the cheek when we met, which was a normal manner of greeting between professional men and women in Australia. If they weren't kissing the male consultants, maybe it was because they were put off by their beards. This suggestion of excessive informality was rattling, and I was disheartened not to be elected to the partnership.

But the story didn't end there. Six months later, I was up for partner again. This time, I made it. As it turned out, my previously criticised familiarity with clients was a strength. Out of the 250 partners, I was one of the top 15 revenue generators my first year, partly due to the fact that clients felt so comfortable with me.

An opportunity may also come back around because you've gained new competencies that make you more desirable. This could be due to experiences at work or skills and knowledge you've acquired while pursuing an outside interest or passion, as Marla Stone saw 40 years into her career.

Getting the job the second time around

Marla Stone is a professor of twentieth-century European history with a focus on the history of fascism, Nazism and genocide. She has been teaching at Occidental College in Los Angeles for nearly three decades. In 1995, she applied for and won the Rome Prize in Post-Classical Humanistic Studies, a year-long fellowship awarded by the American Academy in Rome.

She went to Rome, had a great year, then returned to her academic position. She stayed in touch with the Academy, and even did a few short-term summer fellowships. What she really wanted to do, however, was stay at the Academy in Rome longer, which would be possible if she landed a three-year senior staff leadership position called the Mellon Professor.

The Mellon Professor helps oversee the Rome Prize winners, and acts like 'a dean of humanities', Marla says.[5] It's prestigious and exciting, and after a few years back in Los Angeles, Marla applied for the Mellon Professor role. She was a finalist, but ultimately didn't get the position.

At home in LA, she found herself increasingly worried about the state of democracy in the US. She joined the American Civil Liberties Union (ACLU), a non-profit working to protect individual freedoms outlined in the US Constitution and Bill of Rights. This was not part of her career; she taught history, not current events. But it was a personal passion and something she felt compelled to do. She joined the board of the ACLU of Southern California in 2009. 'I liked the idea of making a really tangible contribution in the present', she says. 'By helping the ACLU flourish, I was contributing to our democracy and the protection of our civil liberties in a real-world, tangible way.'

The ACLU of Southern California has about 100 staff members and a US$14 million annual budget. As Marla's daughter got older, Marla made more time for the ACLU, sitting on committees, then chairing a committee, then moving up to the executive committee, and finally becoming board chair.

For Marla, being on (then chairing) the board felt a little like getting a degree in non-profit management. She was building new skills, like running meetings and committees, learning non-profit board governance and collaborating with people from different backgrounds.

> *This was so different from my day job. In academia, the work is very individual, not really collaborative. Also, the metrics are different. Academia is about publishing and student evaluations. The impact is very long term. At the ACLU, the impact is often immediate, such as in a policy decision, a choice of litigation, an advocacy campaign.*

Then in 2020, she was elected to be the board chair of the ACLU Foundation of Southern California. That same year, her daughter headed to college. Marla applied once again to be the Mellon Professor at the American Academy of Rome.

This time, at the age of 60, she got the coveted, three-year role. She credits her success to stamina, and to the new skills she gained by putting in her time.

> *I think having had high-level administrative and budget experience through my work on the ACLU board, and experience around issues of equity, diversity and inclusion was very appealing to the interview committee. Most academics don't have this management and budget experience. Given the historic moment we're in, my experience with EDI training on the board was important.*

She took a leave of absence from Occidental and headed to Rome in August 2021. Now, speaking from Rome, Marla says her ACLU experience is proving incredibly helpful. 'They just showed me the budget on Friday. Before my time at the ACLU, I would have had no idea what that was. I'd never seen a spreadsheet before.'

(*continued*)

Marla is an example of the power of stamina, not only to remain connected to the Academy in Rome and apply for the role once again, but also to continually find new challenges in a very long working life.

> *We can do a lot of things, even when we think we can't. If you take the risk, you'll see that you can be good at a lot of different things and that you can grow your skill set at any age.*

Power Perspective #3: Remember that you have options

Another stealth stamina-sapper is feeling stuck in a job you don't like, or that no longer challenges you or holds your interest. It's normal to feel under-challenged or stagnant at times, but a prolonged feeling of being trapped in the wrong role can lead to decreased creativity, resignation and depression – and insufficient energy to improve your position and enjoy the other things you love.

First, find out if your dissatisfaction is common at this stage of your career by talking to friends who are at similar levels and perhaps reaching out to your board of directors (which I explain in chapter 3). If so, that may point toward you needing stamina to move through this phase and rise into a role with more autonomy or authority. Recognising that you're experiencing common, early-career discomfort can help you make a conscious choice to stay put for a certain amount of time, which is very different than being 'stuck'.

If the problem is the job, the best way to feel more free is to consider other options. No alternatives in sight? It's time to do some job dating. Seriously.

While people in unhappy marriages generally don't date around in search of a better spouse, if you're frustrated in your job, you definitely should go on some 'job dates' – as in, meetings with people in other firms. Job dating can remind you of your value, which might raise your morale enough to make your current position seem fine. Or, you might realise you want to leave and can. Discovering possibilities gives you an immediate shot of energy and a confidence boost. Suddenly, you find yourself thinking, *Wow! Look how many people want me!* Whereas before you saw an airless cubicle, now you see an open vista.

Job dating can remind you of your value.

A man I know in Singapore, who I'll call Tim Liu, oversees sales in China for his firm. During his seven years in that role, he's built up a team of nearly 50 people. He'd like to try something new, but there are few positions locally with equal pay and authority, and he doesn't want to make a geographic move, so for the time being, he's staying put. He goes on periodic job dates as a way to stay current on new companies, to network and to learn about possibilities for people he knows. He also encourages those on his team to job date as well, partly to test and reaffirm their commitment to their roles. 'I always say to people, "If you're the least bit unhappy or dubious about whether you want to be here, go ahead and talk to other people". It may be surprising to hear that I say this to my own employees. But I'd rather have them happy with me than wondering all the time.'

While you've probably heard the truism that looking for a job is a full-time job, job dating is lighter and more fun. You're just casually scoping out the scene, not seeking commitment. You might discover that your skills are in high demand, as human resources professional Mariabrisa Olivares did when she went on some job dates.

How casual job dating led to career contentment

Originally from Mexico City, Mariabrisa Olivares has lived around the world and speaks several languages. When I met her, she was living in Brazil, overseeing human resources in Latin America for Twitter. From there, she went to London for a job, and then in 2019, she moved from that position to a relatively new tech company

(*continued*)

focused on mobile advertising, called Ogury. Ogury had about 400 employees at the time, but no HR department, which made for a really exciting job for Mariabrisa – at first.

> *I built up a team of 20 people from scratch and put in work structures, a code of conduct and recruitment practices. I was the first and only woman in the C-suite, and I was working with a super smart, young, interesting team. It was incredibly challenging and exciting.*[6]

But near the end of 2020, one of the founders who had left the company returned in an advisory role. Mariabrisa found herself repeatedly disagreeing with him about key HR issues. Eventually, after failing to find common ground, she decided to look around. Recruiters had reached out to her periodically in the past; now she responded.

> *I have strong opinions acquired through my years of experience. A key part of my role is to provide feedback and coaching. I wanted to see if other people would value that and accept it.*

She started doing virtual job dating. HR was an incredibly hot field, she discovered. The pandemic had changed work life completely, and companies of all types were seeking advice on managing people during a crisis. Her specific skills and experiences made her desirable.

> *It's not very common to have someone experienced with US and international markets, who speaks French, English, Spanish and Portuguese. That definitely made my profile attractive. It reassured me that I have a really good skill set.*

She started getting job offers, and reassessing her current situation. Why was she staying put with a boss who didn't value her? During another conflictual conversation, she made a decision. 'I said, "I don't think this is where I want to be. I want to be here for a thousand reasons, but I don't want to be here for this very big one."'

She accepted an offer from Owkin, a tech company focused on developing artificial intelligence and machine-learning solutions for cancer patients. She took a month between the two jobs to travel and get ready for her next adventure.

> *I started interviewing, not with the intention of leaving, but more to reassure myself. When you're in a situation that is causing self-doubt, it's really important to go out and do that.*

If you want to try job dating, you can respond to recruiters, as Mariabrisa did, search on LinkedIn and career sites, check your university's alumni association, attend networking events, review job listings at companies that interest you and reach out to professional connections. If you find yourself in a room with someone from a field or firm that looks intriguing, do what I did when I met Vint Cerf – send an email asking if that firm might consider you. Or ask for a 30-minute informational interview about the company or industry.

Talk to satisfied friends about their jobs. Who feels valued at work and well-paid? Could you move into that field or find a job with that company? The process also forces you to update your social media profile and CV, always good actions to take.

Power Perspective #4: Acknowledge that you are not totally in control

We don't have total control over our careers (even if we follow all the steps in this book). Thinking that we can determine every single thing that happens to us also saps stamina.

Sometimes, real disappointments occur that are out of our control. In my own case, after more than a decade of working successfully as a consultant, I started looking for a new role. I'd been advised by executive recruiters to get out of consulting or be prepared to remain in it forever. Firms want to see that you can run a business, too.

In 1999, I was offered a great new job building and running the international division of the multinational financial services firm Charles Schwab. It was based in San Francisco, so it would entail a huge move for my family back to California. This was no small consideration. I'd just had my second son the year before, so we were looking at moving across the Pacific with two children under the age of four. My husband would also need a job in the States.

Linton also secured a position at Schwab, and we all made the move. It was a big upheaval, and it took us some time to get settled back in California. The boss who hired me left before I arrived, so I no longer had a supporter at the firm. Then, after we'd been there just two years and were finally feeling at home, the firm shuttered its overseas businesses to focus on the US domestic market. I'd given up my partner role at BCG to build Schwab's international division. Now there was no international division.

I was devastated. I knew I was not being rejected and this was just part of the company's strategic decision-making process. But this decision from the top that was out of my control impacted me and my entire family, and meant I had to let go of everyone on my team. It was horrible to have to fire people, to dismantle a team I'd worked so hard to build. (The fact that my job was also disappearing made me feel a bit less guilty, but only a bit.) I enjoy developing opportunities for people, and this was the exact opposite.

The experience turned into a time of real questioning for me. Had I done the right thing by leaving BCG and moving my family to the US? Had I damaged my career with this choice?

Another big question came to me a little late, in retrospect, one that was more positive: Was there an opportunity here I wasn't seeing, such as the chance to take a little time off to stay home with my kids? Or the chance to switch industries or roles?

I wound up taking the severance package offered and staying home for an entire year. I used the first six months to relax, recuperate and be with my sons. Then I started looking for another role. I got a terrific role at Visa after that year out, but it took real stamina for me to move past this disappointment and be ready to start looking again.

My experience is not all that unusual. Firms change course. A great boss leaves. You get layered over. Your company is acquired or folds. When it comes to careers, all kinds of things affect you that are outside your control. As much as developing a sense of agency matters when it comes to supporting stamina, so does realising that you are not totally in control. This is a truth that COVID made very clear – none of us is totally in control of our lives. Hopefully, this is a lesson we can draw on from this incredibly difficult pandemic period.

As much as developing a sense of agency matters when it comes to supporting stamina, so does realising that you are not totally in control.

If you fail to recognise the very real role of luck or chance in challenges that arise, you can feel as if any glitch in your plan is a personal failure, and one that you should have been able to avoid. This refusal to acknowledge fate can lead to overly negative thinking and over-focusing on rejection and failure – mindsets that sap stamina.

You're also not in total control of how things might change in your favour, such as when an opportunity comes back around. Recently, a search firm reached out to me about a great job that didn't interest me. I recommended a friend who was looking around and who I thought would be a perfect fit. The firm reached out to him. He went through a series of interviews, and really enjoyed his conversations with people at the firm. They seemed to like him, too.

Eventually, it came down to just two people, my friend and another guy. The search firm assured my friend that he was the better choice. My friend was really excited. But then he got the bad news: the company chose the other person because he had a more traditional background for the position.

My friend was disappointed. He'd become very interested in this company and the role. But he's an upbeat person in general, and he knew how important it was not to let discouragement sap his stamina or second-guess every conversation he'd had. He also knew that none of us has control over hiring decisions.

Lo and behold! The firm rejected the other candidate in the end, due to something that arose in the final negotiations. The company offered the job to my friend, and he accepted it. He is off to a great start there.

Recognising the role of luck in your life also helps keep you humble as you rise. Taking all the credit for your own good fortune can offend people who have contributed. It also can decrease your own drive. Dan Springer, the CEO of DocuSign, puts it this way:

> ***I do think you have to be in a position where you accept that both good fortune and bad fortune will come your way. You can't get overly down or overly up and get complacent. You have to have that energy to keep charging ahead.***[7]

Springer says that only about a third of the things he's done in his life have turned out exactly how he wanted them to. This is important to remember for all of us. Just as giving in to discouragement when things go wrong can sap stamina, so can assuming you are solely responsible for your bad or good fortune.

For some people, part of stamina is knowing that your work has an impact beyond yourself. Many of us are working in part to support our family, and this responsibility helps push us on. Others may see their leadership role as helping establish a new norm for the next generation. For me, being in a position to help others – by offering advice, making connections, writing recommendations, sharing information about opportunities they might be able to pursue – is a huge part of the pleasure I get from work. Doing this 'extra-curricular' mentoring absolutely contributes to my own career stamina.

Takeaways

- Perseverance + Enthusiasm = Stamina.
- Stamina is a career superpower that can be built. Put your energy into powering up yours.
- Self-care supports stamina. Adopt the mindshift that making time for family, friends and personal interests helps you keep going at work.
- Don't obsess about disappointments, rejections or failures; negative rumination saps stamina. Train your brain to obsess about your success.
- Remember that you always have options. You are not trapped. Do some job dating to remind you of this fact.
- Feeling totally responsible for disappointments – or big wins – saps stamina. Recognise that none of us has total control.

mindshift three

Connection trumps tech savvy...even in tech

Power perspectives in this chapter

- **amass that other critical capital: social capital**
- **show consideration, which is currency in today's hyper-connected, global world**
- **praise often and in public**
- **master the art of feedback.**

Rahul Desai is a superb sales operations guru originally from Austin, Texas. He's a hard worker who has good insights and tends not to draw attention to himself. He's also truly nice, thoughtful, calm and unbelievably thorough. His role involves streamlining processes and providing analytics to accelerate the sales cycle and enable sellers to close more deals. When I met him in 2008, he was working at the Google headquarters in Mountain View, California. He'd previously worked as a consultant, at Dell (a well-known training ground for sales ops) and gotten an MBA. He was quietly grinding away in Mountain View as an analyst, going somewhat unnoticed and underutilised, I thought.

I had just started at Google and was in the process of getting to know the teams in Mountain View and in Asia before moving to Singapore for the second time. I was preparing to go from California to Beijing for a couple of weeks to meet the team in China, work with them on strategy and look at ways to grow the market more quickly. I asked Rahul for some help, and realised right away that he was very talented. I knew he'd be an asset on my Beijing trip, so I asked him to come along.

You definitely get to know the human side of someone when you're travelling together. We found ourselves navigating Beijing together, trying to hail a taxi in pidgin Chinese and bonding over our shared skill of travelling through different climates with a single carry-on bag (a talent honed by having been consultants). Rahul and I spent time together in cars and at group dinners. I shared a little about my family, and told him that I knew some Chinese words because my husband and I had sent both of our boys to a Mandarin immersion school as a way to give them a global perspective. He told me about his girlfriend, who he hoped to marry. We had fun travelling together. The trip also gave me a chance to see how quickly he caught on, how open he was to new ideas, how well he got along with people and how much the team respected his analysis. It also gave him a chance to get to know me.

We were in the Shangri-La Hotel one day, passing through one of those large revolving doors that holds two people in the same section. As I remember it, I turned to him and said, 'Hey, do you want to come join the team in Asia?' I hadn't planned to offer him a job that morning, but it just felt right. He would be an asset to me and to the team if he took the job – and he had to consider it since he was momentarily trapped with me between two walls of glass. I knew he'd be a great addition. I also thought the move would lead to better career opportunities for him because he'd have a chance to shine working for Google in Asia as we built the online sales business across the region.

When we got back to California, I reiterated my offer. It turned out that Rahul had always wanted a chance to work overseas. 'I talked to my girlfriend, and she was open to it', he says. 'There was some negotiation with Google over the details, but I knew I was going to do it. We got married the weekend before I flew out to Singapore, a spur-of-the-moment wedding decision, and she moved out the next month.'[1]

The 'Ah-ha!' of Rahul's story: careers are built by real connection

Why was I comfortable offering him a job after only a few months of working together and a short trip? Because we had formed a real bond. You can't always replicate the kind of personal connection that happens during international travel, of course. But seeing the humanity in those you work with is key to collaborating and getting things done.

The importance of human connection extends beyond hiring decisions. As surprising as it may seem, connecting emotionally with co-workers, employees, bosses and colleagues is a key piece of getting work done and enjoying yourself while doing it. Success depends not just on hard work, but also on our ability to build and maintain genuine relationships throughout our career lives. We benefit from real connections with colleagues, employees and bosses on the job, and with other professionals outside of our current place of work.

Recognising the role of connection is a mindshift for many. Having workers who feel connected to a firm and engaged has been shown to improve profits by as much as 20 per cent.[2]

Power Perspective #1: Amass that other critical capital: social capital

Another term for the strong, trusting relationships that are so important in a career is 'social capital'. Having strong social capital is one of those stealth success strategies; it's essential for thriving in your career, but not always obvious from a résumé. As with financial capital, building and maintaining social capital takes time and attention. But it does *not* mean using people to get ahead, or viewing work relationships in a transactional way. You can accrue social capital in a way that is true to your personality and values.

Some social capital accrues naturally during your interactions at work, of course, but by focusing on building it, you can expand beyond those people you organically meet. You want strong, trusting relationships with your boss, mentors and supporters, as well as with co-workers and other peers, employees and mentees.

Building social capital across departments helps you get things done. If you're in sales and have a good relationship with someone in engineering, for example, and you want that person to spend extra time with a client discussing systems architecture, you'll likely get a better response than you would if you lacked that strong connection. Social capital can also play a part in getting promoted. If you're interested in a job at the next level, and someone within the division who knows you advocates for your work, that support can go a long way toward putting you ahead of others in line for the same promotion.

While social capital is critical to your success, it also matters for those on your team and in your circle. Helping nurture connections for others is part of aiding their development.

Nearly all of us 'drew down' on our social capital during COVID. Part of re-creating a new normal includes rebuilding those connections and continuing to develop new ones. Social capital is harder for dispersed workers to create. In today's global and often virtual work world, with so many people working either far from headquarters or from home, focusing on social capital is particularly important. It takes extra effort to build social capital from afar, but it's doable.

Helping nurture connections for others is part of aiding their development.

Here are three ways to build strong social capital for yourself and others.

1. Seek sponsors at work

A key piece of building social capital is finding an advocate or 'sponsor' within your organisation. A sponsor is someone more senior who looks out for you and your career by mentioning you favourably in meetings, putting you up for a promotion or helping you land a new role within the organisation. This is a genuine relationship – not one with Machiavellian or ulterior motives. But it is a relationship that you *intentionally develop.* Having an advocate within your firm can mean the difference between getting an opportunity you want or watching it go to someone else. It's a normal part of corporate life, and the way many people get ahead in organisations. You can have more than one advocate, but you need at least one.

A sponsor generally starts out as someone who has more experience in the company, and is available to offer you advice and guidance. As the relationship evolves, this person takes an active interest in your career, pushing for you and extending his or her own social capital to campaign for you. The person who hires you is generally your first sponsor. This is your first important relationship within the organisation and one that you nurture by performing well. But your boss might leave or might lack power within the organisation, leaving you without a strong advocate. Be on the lookout for potential sponsors and cultivate them.

Generally, sponsors don't just show up. Even when you feel that you are genuinely liked by those above you, you still have to take steps to turn that goodwill into active sponsorship. When my co-writer, Wendy, moved to New York City about 10 years into her career, she took a job on contract as an associate producer on the weekend morning show at WNBC-TV. She had a supportive boss, but one who lacked power within the newsroom. During her two years on the show, conflicts arose with the production assistants below her and the news director above, and she felt powerless to address them. Then, when she wanted a promotion and more job stability, her boss had nothing to offer. She couldn't figure out her next move.

Looking back on it today, she says that she could probably have cultivated a few sponsors to help with these issues, but never thought to do so.

> ***I had a handful of supporters in the newsroom who all had far more power than I did – a senior reporter I became friends with, three of the news anchors and one of the writers. One of the very senior news anchors actually called me into his office to explain to me the politics of the newsroom and assure me that my struggles weren't personal. I think any of these people would have advocated for me, or maybe helped strategise, if I'd thought to develop the relationship and ask. Instead, I knew they liked me, but I wound up feeling bad about my role and quitting.***

I've been a sponsor for dozens of people over the course of my career and I've seen firsthand how much harder it is to thrive within an organisation without a sponsor. At American Express, after the great boss who brought me in moved on, leaving me with a difficult manager and no one above her advocating for me, I wound up quitting. With a sponsor, I probably would have stayed at the firm.

Later, when I moved from Asia back to the US for the job at Charles Schwab that ultimately ended, my would-be boss left before I even started. I didn't realise how much this would affect me. Before he left, he asked if I wanted to talk to the chief operating officer (COO) for reassurance that my role was still solid, but I didn't take him up on that offer. I was a bit intimidated and I wanted to show my independence. In retrospect, that was a mistake. I should have availed myself of the offer, and taken time to build that connection. During my two years there, I frequently fought to get resources allocated for my division, and to get decisions made. If I'd had a direct connection with the COO or someone else powerful who was pushing for me, I think that period of my career would have gone a lot more smoothly.

5 steps for turning a supporter into a sponsor

Creating sponsors may not come naturally, but it's easy to learn. Here's how:

- **Seek input.** Make an effort to get to know a few senior people at work. Ask for advice from them about how things work at the company, or a better way to get things done or what they think about a specific challenge. Or, if they're working on something interesting, offer to help. Express your appreciation, and try to create a real relationship. If any of those relationships grow into a real connection, and you have a good sense that this person likes you and your work, you've identified a potential sponsor.

- **Share a specific goal.** After a few conversations, let a potential sponsor know about your goals or a specific aim, such as getting a job that has opened up, moving into management or moving overseas. You might say, 'I'd really like to move to the next step. What would you advise me to do?'
- **Be patient.** It takes time for relationships to develop and for your potential sponsor to see your value. Over six months, a year or even more, this person will observe your continued good work and character, and grow more comfortable advocating for you.
- **Keep looking.** If none of the people you've connected with becomes a champion, look around for someone else within your organisation, and once again seek input.
- **Sponsor someone else.** Make sure you advocate for others in your workplace. Bolstering someone else's career isn't a direct step toward gaining a sponsor, but it is part of creating a positive environment and a supportive atmosphere around you.

2. Build a personal board of directors

While supporters inside your organisation provide one type of social capital, you also need ideas and support from people outside your firm, ideally with varied backgrounds and at different stages in their careers. People with different perspectives and expertise can provide novel insights and new knowledge. As with a sponsor, these are relationships you have to intentionally build. I think of it as assembling a 'personal board of directors'.

A personal board of directors is like a team of unpaid career coaches; a half-dozen or so experts available to offer input and advice. Your board can include your parents (if you're someone who still calls your folks for advice, as I sometimes do), but not only them. It takes more than one or two people to provide all the information you need to navigate every issue that will arise in your career. Just as organisations benefit from the skill sets and experiences of a diverse pool of experts, so does your career.

Seeking a range of insights is a proven way to 'function smarter', says science writer Annie Murphy Paul, author of *The Extended Mind: The Power of Thinking Outside the Brain.* 'It's called "cognitive diversity", the idea that in order to see all sides of an issue, you have to solicit the views of a variety of people.' Because we naturally gravitate toward people who think as we do, 'We have to make an intentional effort to seek out people with different points of view to reap that cognitive diversity bonus', says Paul.[3]

Your board of directors can help you notice key areas for growth you might otherwise miss, as Suzy Nicoletti (from chapter 1) learned early in her career.

The benefit of a personal board

About 10 years ago, Suzy Nicoletti was working in sales, and a great job came up for a sales manager at her company. She applied, and because she was performing well in her role, felt pretty optimistic about her chances. The position would mean moving from being a salesperson to a leader, and it seemed like a logical next step to her.

She didn't get the promotion.

This rejection made no sense to her. From her perspective, she'd been doing everything right. 'It didn't fit with the stories I was telling myself', she says.

She sought input from a more senior former colleague in sales. He wasn't as surprised by the rejection as she was. He could clearly see gaps in her work experience she'd missed.

> *He felt that I had amazing personal wins, and great client stories to tell. But I didn't have as many group wins. He didn't see me taking on things that the team or group needed,*

> *or working to bring out the best of different functions. To move into a leadership role, I needed to be thinking more about the team and less about myself.*

This conversation was a turning point for Suzy, inspiring her to start adopting a team focus.

> *It's a classic challenge for a lot of people who want to go from seller to senior seller or leader. Whereas, previously, you're incentivised to hit numbers, now you have to make a big shift and also contribute to the group and constantly make everyone else around you better. I really enjoyed how simply it was put to me by someone from the outside.*

Armed with this new insight, Suzy began focusing more on group successes. She soon landed her first real leadership role – which helped prepare her for the promotion I pestered her to take working for me at Twitter, and eventually for her much larger leadership role as the managing director of Twitter, Australia.

She also began to build a personal board of directors, elevating that former colleague to the first spot on her board (in her mind), and seeking his perspective. She then added others, including a retired banker, a former boss, and her brother, who happened to be a tech executive.

> *That was a fundamental experience for me. I learned that I needed to make sure I had people who were going to see things I wasn't going to see in my everyday work environment. I'd been getting all my ideas and insights from the same group within my company. I realised I was missing richer development perspectives.*

Most people are flattered to be asked for advice, though some won't have time to talk to you. Others may reject your request for input because they think their experience won't be helpful. Don't get discouraged and give up on building a board as many people will want to help. They may be eager to steer people away from pitfalls they've fallen into, or motivated to pay their success forward, especially if they feel fortunate about their own opportunities. I serve on the boards of many people (a fact I discovered when writing this book). While I didn't realise I was 'officially' a board member for all of them, I have long known that supporting others brings me the greatest sense of satisfaction in my career.

6 steps for building a personal board of directors

Assembling a personal board of directors may sound daunting, but it's an easier task than you might think. For one thing, being on someone's board is less work than becoming a mentor, often making a person more willing to do it. Your board members don't even have to know they're on your board; that's just how *you're* seeing *them*. They think they're occasionally waxing profound on their great knowledge. Here's how to develop your board.

- **Go with who you know.** Think about what kind of advice you need, and who among the people you know and respect could give it. This might be a former colleague or supervisor you had a great relationship with, a parent's friend, a parent of a friend, an alumnus from your school, a buddy from your ultimate frisbee team, a former co-worker, a former professor or even someone you've heard speak who seems reasonably accessible (probably not someone as famous as Brené Brown, but maybe someone like me). When I decided that I wanted to become a non-executive director on corporate boards, for example, I reached out to women I knew who were already serving in this capacity.
- **Follow 'warm leads'.** Your personal network may be too limited to really help you grow, especially in the beginning of your career. Look for 'warm leads' – potentially valuable connections of people you know – and ask to be introduced to them. You can find these kinds of connections to others by looking at their LinkedIn page, on alumni websites and/or industry organisations they belong to. If you have your eye on someone with no clear personal connection, look for some

shared experience, however tenuous. I recently had someone reach out through social media who highlighted the fact that we were alumni of the same company (though we didn't work there at the same time). She wrote an emotional plea for help finding a company open to diversity. To me, that was a request worth answering, and I made the time to talk to her.

- **Make a specific request.** Reach out by email, phone or in person (if it's someone you see regularly). Share your genuine admiration for some aspect of this person's work, then ask for 15 minutes of their time to talk about a few career questions you have, or for a more general informational interview.
- **Keep the conversation going.** It's up to you to build this relationship. Generally, it's a good idea to email or call quarterly to ask if they have time for a check-in by phone or video conference or to join you for coffee, if this feels appropriate. If you run into a board member naturally at work events (or at the dining table, if it's an in-law), ask to sit down for a career chat.
- **Be interested in them.** Your board members should be people you like and are interested in as human beings. Show this interest by asking about their projects or passions during your quarterly check-ins. Inquiring about the amazing things in someone else's life helps maintain and develop a real relationship, and prevents it from feeling transactional. You want to strike a balance between showing genuine interest in your sponsor and getting the help you need, while also respecting their time.
- **Be on a board.** Make sure to pay it forward by joining someone else's board and making time to give advice when asked. This is the best way to honour the efforts of those who have helped you along the way.

You are also a valuable connection for your board members, and have something to contribute to them in return. I recently replied to a young woman who had reached out on social media for guidance about a difficult work situation. I provided some insight and moral support. I learned, through the conversation, that she happened to know a prominent Singaporean executive I'd always wanted to meet. She introduced me to him. See? People can benefit their board members in very real ways.

3. Connect with colleagues while giving back

Social capital could also be called 'trust in action', and one surprisingly effective way to strengthen trust among colleagues is to give back to the community together. Many people today want to feel that their company is connected to a mission they support and is a good corporate citizen, contributing to the community. Research on millennial workers and Gen-Z, in particular, shows that they prioritise ethical leadership, diversity and inclusion, and companies that care about their well-being.[4]

Many companies create regular, one-off opportunities for team members to volunteer at. People get the day off to participate, and generally show up dressed in the company T-shirt and throw themselves into the activity of the day. Group volunteering can bring out parts of yourself you don't normally express at work and highlight the company's brand in the community. These activities help define the culture of the organisation and set the tone, and can generate a very strong sense of identity and belonging for employees.

Volunteering together can also strengthen social capital within teams and across the organisation in very tangible ways, as Bala Subramaniam, a human resources professional with two decades of experience in the field, discovered when he helped organise Twitter Singapore's Friday for Good events.

Friday for Good

At Twitter, people in offices across the world volunteer at local organisations on a specific Friday a few times a year. Bala co-led a cross-functional team to organise the Singapore office's participation. The first activity they created was a day of volunteering at a food distribution centre called Willing Hearts. Almost everyone from the office – about 30 people at the time – came to help prepare and distribute food to the needy.

One group chopped and cleaned the vegetables, one group cooked and one group drove the meals to the people. A lot of people don't cook at home in Singapore, so this was stepping outside their boundaries.[5]

For him, that one event felt transformative. 'It left such a profound impact on me that I still go there and volunteer on weekends', he says.

It also inspired him to help organise a second Friday for Good, this one visiting elderly residents at an assisted-living facility called Lee Ah Mooi Old Age Home. Again, most of the team participated in what turned out to be an even stronger team-building outing than the first.

While at the old-age home, some of the team members decided on the spur of the moment to put on a variety show to entertain the residents. Pretty much everyone joined in.

People who had never danced at an office dinner, no matter how crazy things got, came up and started dancing with their colleagues to entertain this audience of mostly Singaporean Chinese in their eighties. We had people from all different countries, and they sang songs from their hometowns, in their languages. Once you saw the elders responding and being so happy, you couldn't sit down. I joined a group that did a Bollywood song. I would never do that ordinarily. And we were all sober.

Back at the office, the show became a shared memory that brought people closer.

People would say, 'Hey, remember that song we sang? It was so embarrassing!' Or, 'Oh you were terrible.' 'Yes, and you were terrible, too.' And then we'd all laugh together and go out to lunch. Every group that did something together wound up hanging out after. If you saw three people singing at the old-age home, you'd later see them taking coffee breaks

(*continued*)

together. People who danced together wound up being great friends.

This bond created social capital.

Teams became more willing to work together more and help each other out. It's not clear that this was the event that tipped it, but the relationship was now beyond personal interest. It was more selfless, and not so transactional.

For the third event, an in-office auction to raise money for Singapore Community Chest, team members brought in items they no longer needed, such as music systems or tennis rackets, and auctioned them to co-workers. Twitter matched the amount raised. Once again, this volunteer group effort sparked creativity.

On the day of the event, people started auctioning their time. They'd offer a voucher for 'Me Coming to Wash Your Windows'. Or an hour of training on Excel. A [young woman] from Russia said she would organise a Russian dining experience for two. We printed these offers on cards, with our branding and logo, so they were tangible. Later, when people redeemed their vouchers, it brought back the experience of the day, and contributed to more relationship building.

These experiences sold Bala on the wide-ranging benefits of bringing people together for a purpose.

The bond created transcends the activity. It also demolishes hierarchy. The vice-president and a recent grad are standing together, chopping vegetables. As a leader, if you don't do this, you're missing something big. That sense of doing something for a greater good gives people a stronger unifying purpose than team-building activities or team lunches. It's far stronger than what you can incentivise with money. You're taking something from them – their time, their effort, even their old guitars – but what they get back is a sense of belonging, purpose and a feeling of contributing to the greater good.

Power Perspective #2: Consideration is currency

I had a funny experience at a hip Sydney café recently that made me think about how 'old fashioned' does not necessarily mean 'unworthy' or 'not valuable'.

I always order decaf lattes with whole milk when I'm out for coffee (something my friends scoff at as not 'real' coffee at all). When the server listed the types of milk available, she offered soy, oat, almond and coconut, but nothing resembling the white, creamy stuff that I grew up drinking. I said, 'Can I just have milk-milk, the dairy kind, like from a cow?'

'No, we don't have that', she said.

I just wanted a traditional latte. Not an option. Fine. I ordered my coffee with a dairy alternative and enjoyed it (almost) as much. Now, I'm not sharing this story to make a point about veganism (or lack thereof). Rather, it made me reflect on the fact that with so much that is new and improved all around us, it's easy to forget that certain old standbys still have a role. When it comes to career, I'm talking about manners. Yes, those 'old-fashioned' behaviours your grandma tried to teach you.

Manners may seem like a small point to focus on – and they often are small actions – but they make a huge difference when it comes to building and maintaining connections in your career.

We all make an effort to mind our manners in our personal lives. Bringing back a small gift from a trip for a friend who watched your dog is good manners. Calling a sibling to say how much you enjoyed the dinner he made for the family reunion is another example of being polite. These small gestures increase our positive regard for those in our immediate circle and affirm our appreciation and connection.

Manners make a huge difference when it comes to building and maintaining connections in your career.

The same is true for those at work but, unfortunately, when it comes to our careers, many of us forgo these normal acts of consideration. We can be so focused on achieving a goal and the obstacles before us that we forget to express appreciation for those helping us overcome them. We point out employees' or colleagues' mistakes, or highlight problems, but fail to acknowledge a job well done.

Rudeness at work may be on the rise. Two Portland State University researchers conducted a meta-analysis of office incivility[6] and found it growing in the virtual workplace since the start of the pandemic. Examples of incivility include colleagues criticising each other in public, texting or emailing during meetings and ignoring or interrupting co-workers. The study authors said that something simple, like not getting enough sleep, can spark uncivil behavior, which can then spiral.

This is happening at a time when consideration matters more than ever due to today's hyper-connected, often-dispersed, global work environment. 'More and more, we long for business relationships where we're treated well', says applied behavioural science expert Amy Alkon, author of *Good Manners for Nice People Who Sometimes Say F*ck*, and other books.[7]

> ***At the root of manners is empathy, caring about how your behaviour makes others feel. We've evolved to notice people who don't treat us with respect, who are freeloaders, who don't do their share of the work. Very little has changed in terms of the way our minds work.***

In other words, if you don't make a point of showing your appreciation, concern and respect for others, they'll feel it, and respond accordingly, perhaps with damaging consequences down the line. Disrespect, rudeness and bad manners in general, if unchecked, can negatively affect the mental health, morale and productivity of employees. As a leader, it's important to establish a politeness policy and no tolerance for bullying in person or online.

One impressive leader I know in Asia created a welcome deck specifically on manners to share with new employees. The slideshow highlights her expectations for behaviour, including politeness, consideration and honesty. It also warns about backstabbing or gossip.

Here are three key ways to mind your manners at work.

1. *Thank people for their efforts*

Well, you might think, I'm getting paid to go to work. So are my employees and colleagues. I don't need to thank these people for doing their job.

Yes, you do, if you want to have a positive, productive work environment. A small effort to express appreciation, such as sending a thank you note or text, increases your connection to colleagues, just as it does in your personal life. Alkon says:

> ***We have this myth that things are created by this lone genius in their garret, but most achievements are collaborative. The help or advice someone gives you might lead you to tweak your idea in a way that makes it work. We owe them credit and thanks.***

Thanking someone for their work conveys the message that their efforts matter. This can increase their willingness to prioritise your projects, which translates into more success for you and your team. The person feels a sense of investment in your aims, and is more likely to keep you and your team in mind when considering new products or projects. They are more inclined to help with your clients or customers.

Giving thanks also boosts people's sense of meaning at work, which matters, especially for millennials and Gen-Z. Even though we all work for a pay cheque, no one wants to feel like a wage slave. As numerous studies show,[8] a sense of meaning and purpose contribute to longevity, health, wellbeing and happiness. The positive impact of meaning lasts longer than the temporary boost we get from other pleasures, like buying a new pair of shoes. 'The good news is, *"meaningfully ever after"* seems to have legs',[9] as Alkon puts it.

As you move on in your career, you may find yourself reflecting on those who helped you rise. It's worth taking the time to send a retroactive thank you. I did this in 2017. I'd gone from my first tech job at Google onto Twitter and then Cloudflare. I was thinking about how it all started, and the role that Vint Cerf at Google played 10 years earlier when I'd first met him in San Francisco at my old Visa job. I decided to send him another thank you note, letting him know what an impact he'd had on me.

He responded, saying he was pleased to receive my note and to hear that my career had blossomed. I felt good about taking the time to do something nice for someone else, and while I'm no longer looking for a job, it's always valuable to remain connected to others.

I advise people to make a weekly habit of thinking about who has helped you or done a great job, and thanking them. Mark it as a recurring item on your calendar. Scheduling 15 minutes to send appreciative emails may have more impact than anything else you do all week; that's how much this simple act helps strengthen connections. It's also a type of gratitude practice, reminding you of what's going well in your career. It's like a 15-minute US Thanksgiving holiday every week (without the turkey). As a leader, making a habit of thanking others helps create a culture of consideration or 'trickle-down humanity', as Alkon calls it.

It can also be a lot of fun. I love to collect small items from around the region when I travel. During my years running APAC for Google, Twitter and Cloudflare, I kept these little items in a drawer. Whenever someone went the extra mile for me or for the region I ran, I'd send an often-goofy, small token of appreciation from the area, and a hand-written thank you on a sticky note with my signature curly-hair icon. I've sent handkerchiefs printed with sumo wrestlers from Japan, elephant-shaped candles from Cambodia, key rings from the Sydney Opera House. Everything cost less than about three dollars, and I paid for them personally. (Choosing very inexpensive, novelty items highlighted my effort to connect through this gesture and eliminated any worry about the appropriateness of accepting gifts.) These fun, silly (tacky?) expressions of appreciation let the other person know how grateful I was – and they helped ensure that others kept our region top-of-mind.

2. *Follow through on commitments*

Follow-through is another old-fashioned yet extremely relevant piece of corporate consideration. If someone asks you for an introduction or to share information, and you agree to do it, make sure you do. Good follow-through builds your reputation for being reliable, a quality managers look for. Poor follow-through, on the other hand, can start to erode people's confidence in you. Managers and colleagues may start asking others for help instead of you, and giving them the opportunities you want. In other areas of your life, lack of follow-through can have serious consequences – such as letting (what turns out to be) a serious medical condition grow rather than following up on a doctor's referral, or never getting around to investing your money.

Like giving thanks, it's worth developing the habit of follow-through. As a recent study published in the *Behavioral Science & Policy* journal shows, simple interventions can dramatically improve your follow-through skills. These steps include making concrete, specific plans for when you'll do something, and scheduling it. Another intervention is adding prompts on your calendar or phone to remind you of your plans. 'Planning prompts seem to work because scheduling tasks makes people more likely to carry them out. They also help people recall in the right circumstances and in the right moment that they need to carry out a task', the study authors write.[10] And if someone makes a request, and you are pretty sure you're not going to do it? It's better to politely decline a request than to accept it and fail to deliver.

3. Show up

Showing up is an important type of consideration and one that conveys – or detracts from – respect for others. Showing up for meetings and calls is a way of recognising that others matter, and so does their time. We all have to cancel at some point, but don't do it three times in a row to the same person or to someone who has gone out of their way to make an appointment. If you forget about a meeting until after it's over, apologise profusely, and make sure you go out of your way to accommodate this person the next time.

Showing up also means being fully present when you're there (rather than on your phone, something I admit I'm guilty of at times). Even if you consider yourself a great multitasker, being on the phone answering text messages or sending tweets during a meeting conveys the message that the person speaking is not worth your full attention. It's rude and distracting. Though I will say that when I was at Twitter, creators of a key application of mass distraction, we encouraged people to tweet at conferences and whenever else something happened that was remotely shareable, so some variation does exist in terms of what's considered rude. In general, as Alkon says, it's important to show respect by visibly paying attention.

> ***Are you a doctor doing a liver transplant in the next twenty minutes? Okay, you can be on your phone. Everyone else, put your phone ... Otherwise, no one is paying attention to the meeting, and anything could get said. When you're on your phone, that tells the other person that they don't really matter, or that they matter like thirty percent, because the other seventy percent is on your phone.***

Paying full attention to a person who is speaking is a form of generosity, 'a generosity of spirit', Alkon says. 'Listening tells us we're important, that you respect us and that you're treating us with respect. Attention is a form of respect.'

Okay, maybe you can't help it. While mental health experts debate whether or not phone addiction is a real thing, there are definitely similarities in behaviour between people who seem unable to put down their phone and those with a diagnosed gambling addiction.[11] These behaviours include an inability to control the behaviour, withdrawal if the phone is not around, relapse after breaking the habit, and even serious negative consequences from overuse (like losing friends or failing to be promoted at work because managers don't think you care). If you're really challenged in this regard, you may want to seek professional help, such as cognitive behavioural therapy or a digital detox program. At work, you can try suggesting, as Alkon says, that everyone puts their phone in a basket during meetings, and see if you can establish this as the new norm. At the very least, put your phone in your bag (and sit on your hands to keep it there, if you must).

Power Perspective #3: Praise often, and in public

As with minding your manners, it's very easy to forget to praise those around us in a work setting. But praise gives people energy and confidence, promotes good performance and helps create connection. Frequent, deserved praise creates a culture of positive reinforcement and is part of what lands companies on the top of 'Best Places to Work' lists. It's a good skill to develop, whatever level you are at in your career. I'm not suggesting you lavish others with manipulative, artificial or obsequious compliments, but rather make a habit of noticing and acknowledging the good work around you.

During lockdown, we all experienced what it feels like to go without the kind of spontaneous positive feedback that comes when you work together. Many of us also experienced how easy it is to dwell on the negative when working alone. As more workplaces become hybrid, praise can matter even more. It's very hard to feel connected and appreciated by those you don't regularly see.

Many of the best companies incorporate time for public praise into their weekly operations. Cloudflare's virtual 'town halls' – internal meetings that include employees from around the globe – end with slides thanking specific employees and teams. These weekly shout-outs from and about employees help create a sense of being appreciated and noticed, feelings that motivate people and inspire loyalty. Praise and recognition are important parts of doing business.

At Mediacorp, Singapore's national media conglomerate, workers at all levels are asked to give 'kudos' to fellow employees who have demonstrated the company's core values of respect, teamwork and drive. These collegial call-outs are registered on the company's Intranet 'Kudos Hall of Fame'. Managers can give 'super kudos', which include a cash bonus and a public mention during the town hall. Google also encourages employees to praise each other, offering 'peer bonus' funds for employees to give to colleagues who've been particularly helpful to them.

You might worry that it's risky to highlight the good work of a colleague who might one day want the same promotion you seek. But praising peers helps create a positive environment in general. Complimenting the work of others reflects well on you, in part because it conveys real confidence. You're not afraid to share the credit, and others notice this. Also, the people you praise will probably return the favour, so your successes will likely get noticed without you having to boast about them. (You do need to make sure your good work gets seen, even if you have to promote it yourself. More on this in chapter 4.)

Okay, sure: sometimes being on the receiving end of praise in a public forum can feel a little embarrassing. But it also feels good, and can make a real impact. While we'd like to believe that all good work gets noticed, this isn't really the case, especially for those who work in supporting roles. People can see the work of the star salesperson or programmer at a tech firm. But the star accountant in a non-accounting firm can labour in obscurity for years. Most people will have no idea how good they are or even think about their role. They need people (like you) to brag about them.

As a leader, it's part of your job to make sure others see your team shine.

Rahul Desai has become a great manager over the years, moving from that job at Google on to Facebook and into various leadership roles. He stayed in Singapore for nine years, and then moved back home to Texas. To help his people rise, he makes a point of highlighting their contributions by name when talking to the chief revenue officer (CRO) or CEO.

> ***From that first experience in Singapore, I learned how important it is to make sure to highlight the work of others. When I moved to Facebook in Singapore and led a team, I flew back to California regularly for that job. I made sure to speak about my team's work when I was at headquarters, and to advocate for them to take on global projects that were likely to get recognised.***

As Rahul has seen, repeatedly calling out specific accomplishments of employees helps build a case for their promotion, which is especially valuable if higher-ups don't interact with them in person. By using his social capital to share the specific contributions of individuals with those higher up, he helps leaders see who's having an impact in the organisation.

> ***I'll say, 'Lauren produced this', when sharing a success with the CRO. Lauren doesn't get seen by the CEO, so it's an opportunity for me to give her visibility. Over time, people will be like, 'Huh. I keep hearing Lauren behind projects that are successful'. By the time I say to the CRO, 'I think we should promote Lauren', he'll say, 'Oh, of course. You're coming to me every week with this new thing she's created'.***

As a leader, praising people on your team reflects well on you. As Rahul says:

> ***One thing I've learned in my career is that what speaks loudly for a manager is not what the manager can directly claim they built, but rather what I'm producing via my team. It's implied I was involved.***

Power Perspective #4: Master the art of feedback

Giving feedback is a challenge for many first-time managers. How you do it affects whether or not others receive it well, and what kind of relationship you develop. As you move up in your career, and more of your daily interactions at work are with people you manage, developing good feedback skills becomes an essential part of creating good connections. But just telling someone what they're doing wrong does not generally improve a relationship or the person's performance, as a young man I recently advised discovered.

Using positive feedback to inspire improvement

A man who had recently been promoted to a manager position came to me for advice about giving feedback. A new hire he managed was not performing well. The manager had told him specifically what needed to change, several times, but the employee had failed to improve. Instead of acting on this manager's input, he seemed to be growing dejected by it. 'Is it my body language?' the manager asked. Could that be why the employee wasn't responding?

I suspected the problem was one of negative override: the employee was focused on his failings, and losing his confidence and mojo. The manager's goal should be to help him get it back. People do well when they feel good about themselves and supported in their role.

(continued)

For starters, he needed to connect with this guy on a human, emotional level, and let him know that he wanted him to do well. I asked, 'Do you think he knows you're on his side?' He'd just joined the company and was probably distressed by his poor performance. I suggested that, in addition to outlining the need for change, the manager should tell him he wanted him to succeed, or perhaps ask him if he thought he was on his side.

This can be an uncomfortable question to pose, I know. If an employee admits that they don't feel like you're rooting for them, you have to face your own need for improvement as a manager. But whether he presented it as a fact or a question, it would be a good place to start. He could say, 'I'm giving you this feedback because I want you to succeed, not because I'm trying to push you out.'

He could then explain why his success mattered to him, both personally and professionally. For one thing, the company had already invested in him; it would be far better for the firm if the role worked out. Second, it would reflect better on him as a manager if he helped this employee succeed. Third, on a personal level, he liked the guy and wanted him to do well. These points were all true, so it would be good to share them.

My second suggestion was that he highlight the employee's successes, even if they were small or in areas where he was otherwise floundering. Saying, 'That was great!' could help build his confidence and inspire him to repeat those productive actions. In this way, highlighting the positive helps build it. If someone's confidence is low, and you let them know you support them and you find something to praise, you can inspire real improvement in performance.

He tried this approach, and the guy's mood and attitude improved. He felt better, and tried harder. Ultimately, he left the job. But the experience helped him recognise some of his strengths and enabled the new manager to improve his feedback skills, making it a win for both of them.

When it comes to detailing exactly how an employee is falling short, some managers struggle. They don't want to sound critical or make the person mad at them. Kim Scott, author of *Radical Candor: How to Be a Kick-Ass Boss Without Losing Your Humanity*, has a term for failing to give needed constructive feedback: ruinous empathy. This is when a leader cares deeply about an employee but is afraid to challenge that person directly. The leader never tells the person that improvement is needed, and the person can wind up being fired without ever knowing there was a performance problem in the first place.

People who are very agreeable, as a personality trait, can struggle the most with giving negative feedback, says psychology professor Art Markman.

> ***Agreeableness is driven, in part, by a need to be liked. If I criticise you, you're not going to like me at that moment. So they'll often soft-pedal it, use passive voice or try not to assign blame. They'll say things like, 'I know you tried really hard, but...' Or, 'You're a valuable contributor, but...' Then they don't actually come out and say what happened.***

For new leaders who are nervous about delivering criticism (and may have trouble sleeping the night before a performance evaluation), Markman recommends what he calls the 'XYZ model' of delivering negative feedback.

> ***You say, 'You did X. It resulted in Y. Next time I want you to do Z instead.' Don't attempt to analyse their motives. Just stick to desired outcomes. There should be a specific statement of what you want the person to do in the future. It takes practice, but what's nice about this formula is that you can learn it. You can just memorize it. It's a great way of delivering criticism.***

Of course, feedback goes both ways – you give some; you get some. Receiving feedback well determines whether or not you gain from it. It also affects your connection with managers and bosses.

As Suzy Nicoletti learned when she didn't land an expected promotion, feedback from those more senior can help you gain needed perspective – if you are open to it and can take it as a learning moment. It's easy to get defensive when you're on the receiving end of feedback, but this response prevents you from gaining useful information that will help you do better.

As a leader, you need constructive feedback from your team to help you continually improve. You should seek this input. I recently saw a LinkedIn post on feedback from Kim Scott that I really liked: 'When GIVING feedback, try to focus on the good stuff and give more praise than criticism. When GETTING feedback, solicit criticism, not praise.'[12] Scott even offers a 'feedback ratio' for leaders. She suggests that, as a manager, you give three or five or seven points of praise for each constructive critique, but when asking for feedback, invert that ratio to 10-to-one (critique to praise), or even more.

By learning to see feedback as a tool for improvement, you can capitalise on this important, regular work interaction. Feedback is so valuable that I recommend people go out of their way to ask for it, and even solicit feedback from colleagues. If someone sees you give a sales pitch, for example, ask for input immediately afterward – both what you did well and what you might do better. This can be valuable feedback that no one else is as able to provide.

Feedback is another important form of connection. As with other aspects of connection, you can develop your feedback skills to help you rise and thrive.

Takeaways

- Amass that *other* critical capital, social capital – as in, genuine, trusting relationships and goodwill – throughout your career.
- Look for a few supportive, senior staff members to become 'sponsors' of your career and advocate for you within your firm. Sponsors are critical to rising and thriving in today's competitive work world.
- Assemble a personal board of directors outside your firm. Like companies, we all need a range of insights to help us grow.
- Mind your manners! Consideration is currency in today's often-dispersed, hyper-connected world. Small moves matter – thanking others, showing up, making good on commitments, and being present when you're with someone (rather than on your phone).
- Praise others often and in public (when they deserve it)
- Master the art of feedback – both giving it and getting it. Adopt the mindshift that receiving feedback is a tool for personal growth.

mindshift four

You are in a relationship with your career: Nurture it

Power perspectives in this chapter

- keep your eye on your prize
- make sure your good work gets seen
- fight back (skilfully) when wronged
- set boundaries to protect all of your relationships.

I was playing badminton with a coach at an indoor facility in Botany Bay, Australia, when I noticed a young woman on the courts who looked like she might play at about my level, which I consider 'permanent advanced beginner'. (I played badminton in junior high, but then not again until my forties.) I don't stand a chance against serious badminton athletes, but I love the sport. Naturally, I had to meet this woman, perhaps the only badminton player in all of Sydney who wouldn't beat me 21-0 every time.

I approached her and suggested we play a match. She agreed.

We began meeting weekly at the courts while I was in Australia. I learned a lot about this young woman, Katrien, between sets. Originally from Belgium, she is nomadic and ambitious, and unafraid to share her views – qualities I relate to (and share).

She was working at a leading tech company in Sydney. One day, during a break between sets, she told me that she had nascent job offers with two other companies. She liked her current firm, but she wanted to rise and her boss refused to promote her. She didn't want to leave her company, but one of these other offers included greater responsibility and a raise, while the other would give her a much bigger title. After our final game that day, I asked her to tell me about the two options. She talked for a full five minutes about one, a tech company where a former boss had gone, a person who would be a strong advocate for her (an important factor, as you know from chapter 3). But she'd asked people at that company about the culture and gotten mixed reviews. The other company was a very young start-up offering a great title but a lot of risk. She barely talked about this second company, which made me doubt her interest in it. When I asked, she thought about it for a minute and then admitted that it wasn't really an appealing offer. This realisation allowed her to stop considering that role, which freed up mental space for weighing her real options.

She told me that she suspected her current boss would finally step up and offer her a promotion if she accepted a position at another firm.

'Would you rather be promoted where you are, or take a new job?' I asked.

'I don't want to take a promotion where I am if it only comes after I threaten to leave', she said.

'Don't be ridiculous', I said. (No one has ever accused me of soft-pedalling my opinions.) I understood her desire for her boss to see the value of her contributions on his own, rather than only after she threatened to leave, but her *real aim* was to move into a position she liked with a higher title and salary. She wanted a promotion; she did not also need proof of her boss' undying appreciation.

'Your boss hasn't promoted you already partly because he hasn't had to', I said. 'If he offers you the job now, assume it's because you deserved it all along. If you'd prefer to stay where you are than leave, you should take it.'

The 'Ah-ha!' of Katrien's story: Like a partner, your career responds to what you do

Katrien had three options before her. The outcome was not set in stone. It was up to her to make the right choice for herself, and not let her frustration with her boss confound her aims. The next step at work – and her satisfaction with her career – would depend on her actions, on what she did to stay happy and fulfilled.

People often talk about 'climbing the corporate ladder', as if your career is a static object, unresponsive to your actions. It leans against a wall; you climb. But your career is not an inanimate object. It functions more like a partner, reacting and adapting to what you do. Your career is a relationship you build – not an object you buy at the hardware store and shove in a back closet until a problem arises.

You have to pay attention to your career relationship, work on it and protect it. This may sound like bad news – yes, your career is *another* relationship that needs your attention. The good news is that a great career relationship, like a great personal relationship, does not depend on you getting exactly what you want all the time, which is impossible. Rather, you build a great career relationship by adopting certain attitudes and actions that help it flourish.

This is not to say that your career relationship must be an all-consuming passion. We work to earn a living, but in recent decades, the idea has arisen that a good income isn't good enough; you should also be passionate about your work. There can be a lot of pressure for your career to express your identity or fulfil your sense of self. While some people derive most of their pleasure and identity from work, plenty of perfectly happy people are not in an intense love affair with this specific job or that. Don't ruin your relationship with your career by expecting it to feel like a deep soul connection if it doesn't.

Passion is a high bar, and not the right one for everyone. It's an unfair expectation to put on a job that also gives you a pay cheque. As author Kim Scott said:

> ***[T]he world may not pay you for the things that you're great at and that you love to do. There's nothing wrong with working hard to earn a paycheck that supports the life you want to lead.***

Scott suggests asking yourself if the job will offer 'the resources – meaning time, money, and energy – to pursue my passions?'[1]

Even if you do love your job, expecting non-stop ardour is risky because it suggests that your career will fill all your needs, which it can't. While your career can fulfil you in so many ways, it can't do everything. Just as a romantic relationship can enhance your life but not address every single interest you have, so, too, can your relationship with your career be fulfilling and rewarding, and yet still require you to look outside work for things you want to do and learn. Outside interests are how we create a full life, and they help us remain fresh and excited about our work.

Here's how to create a great relationship with your career.

Power Perspective #1: Keep your eye on *your* prize

Some time during my first five years of working, I had an epiphany: *no one is going to take care of me except for me.*

This reality is not so obvious at first. It's not what we're used to. As children, our parents generally *did* take care of us. It was their job to help us grow and succeed (even if we have some complaints about exactly *how* they went about it). We're accustomed to having the important people above us think about us and genuinely care about our success in life.

In life-before-career, merit generally gets rewarded. At school and university, if you perform well, you get good grades. In sports, if you score a goal, your team gets the point. It's very easy to assume that in 'real life', this same general reality holds true.

It doesn't. At least not consistently.

While organisations generally bill themselves as meritocracies, in reality, it's hard to define individual merit in a business setting. There are many moving parts, and leaders can't consistently measure and evaluate all of the various aspects of every single person and grant promotions accordingly. People above you are focused on their own work and positions and are unlikely to notice all the details of yours. While a good boss should advocate for you and help you strategise to meet your goals, you can't always rely on this. The truth is, if you want to rise and thrive at work, you have to look out for yourself. Even within great organisations, if you don't identify your goals and ask for them directly, you probably won't get them.

In Katrien's case, my advice was to figure out her main objective, and avoid sabotaging her success by having a reaction to her boss that came, in part, from an unrealistic expectation of what the firm should do for her. Between matches during subsequent badminton sessions, I encouraged her to consider her various interests and rank them. You can't get everything you want all at once; it's important to figure out your priorities, to keep your eye on your prize.

The truth is, if you want to rise and thrive at work, you have to look out for yourself.

While Katrien had originally spoken with great excitement about going to a new company, she eventually realised that her real desire was to return to Europe to be closer to her family. Europe was her first priority, followed by not taking a huge risk (like on an unknown, fledgling company). After that, she cared about getting a raise and then, finally, a better title. Figuring out her order of desires helped her decide what to do.

She took a promotion with her current firm to oversee Belgium, the Netherlands and Luxembourg, and moved to Europe. She managed to refocus on her own aims, rather than getting derailed by inconsequential details. This focus is critical when it comes to developing a great relationship with your career.

Keeping your eye on your prize includes being true to your values, behaving in your career with the same honesty and integrity you bring to your personal life. (This is the opposite of a *Sopranos*-like ethos of being nice at home then knocking off enemies at work.) Keeping the same principles in both domains lets you rise and thrive without internal conflict.

While I do not believe you have to step on others to get what you want, you do need to step *forward* when opportunities arise. This may feel uncomfortable at times, a fact that a man who I'll call Matteo had to overcome.

Seizing an opportunity when it arises

Matteo, who works at a large firm in Singapore, told me that his boss had been fired unfairly. When I asked if he was interested in his boss's job, he baulked. He didn't want to be an 'ambulance chaser', capitalising on someone else's misfortune. What kind of person would that make him?

'Would you *like* the position?' I asked.

'Well, yes. But it feels wrong to go for it', he said.

I understood his discomfort, but his boss's boss was going to have to hire someone new anyway. While the dismissal felt unfair and disappointing, it did open up an opportunity. It certainly was appropriate for Matteo to consider whether he wanted to pursue it.

In the immediate term, his boss's boss was missing a key manager. Matteo was perfectly positioned to help fill the void and show how well he could respond to crises. I suggested he approach his boss's boss and offer assistance. He needn't set up a meeting about the now-vacant role as if he'd mapped out his own future in it, but could wait for the next weekly, one-on-one conversation and make some genuinely helpful suggestions for dealing with the crunch. Then pitch in to act on them. His boss's misfortune was also a chance to build his own reputation within the company and position himself for a more senior role.

Like Matteo, people often worry about the *how* of an opportunity. They fret that positioning themselves for a promotion will look greedy or callous. They ask themselves, 'Did I really get this on my own merit?' They may suffer from 'impostor syndrome', secretly suspecting they don't deserve their rewards. In recent years, I've heard people worry about opportunities that may have arisen, in part, due to current pressure on organisations and boards to improve gender diversity and inclusion. I've heard people say, 'If I'm only being offered this now because of my ethnicity, race, or gender, they're not valuing me for what I can deliver. Maybe I shouldn't take it.'

You should take opportunities that arise (if you want them), and do a good job. In the case of diversity and inclusion, your success helps open doors for others, which is a huge added bonus that should help appease any discomfort about why you got in. In all cases, what matters is landing a job you want and have a good shot at succeeding in, not how or why it got offered to you, as long as it's legal and ethical.

Keeping your eye on your prize also means negotiating for what you want. This can be particularly challenging for people at the beginning of their career. When Emily Rubin (chapter 2) was offered her first job in San Francisco, she considered rejecting it due to the low salary. But salary is part of a negotiation and it's almost always worth a try to ask for more, if you want it. I advised Emily to find out if this was their best offer. She was hesitant. Today, she says:

> ***I was afraid to ask for a higher salary. It was my first job offer after many months of trying to get a job, and I didn't want to lose it. And I didn't want to make a bad impression.*** [2]

Asking for a better starting salary does not make a bad impression, as I assured her. Nor will a company retract an offer just because you've countered with a reasonable request for a higher salary, one that is in line with that of similar positions and/or based on real reasons, such as a competitive offer elsewhere.

Emily finally agreed to try. 'I tried to make the conversation polite and logical, and to use professional terms like "relocation expenses", "cost of living", and "entry-level salaries at other tech jobs".'

The firm did not budge.

> ***They were like, 'We don't negotiate entry-level salaries'. That was it. I didn't lose the offer. They said we could discuss a raise in a year. I was sad not to get more money, but the conversation and aftermath weren't negative at all.***

Salary negotiation is one area where young women, in particular, hesitate. Sometimes well-meaning advisers contribute to this reluctance, as another young, recent Emory graduate, Davida Halev, experienced.

Don't be afraid to ask

Davida Halev graduated from Emory University and sought a job in the growing plant-based food industry. After not landing any offers, she took an unpaid, remote internship at a start-up in San Francisco called Black Sheep Foods, which was working to create a plant-based alternative to ground lamb meat. After her three-month internship, the company offered Davida a full-time position.

She was excited. But she'd also secured an offer from another plant-based food company based in North Carolina, where she's from and where the cost of living is significantly lower. The salary was the same, but worth more in North Carolina than in California.

She really wanted to work for Black Sheep Foods, but she also wanted more money. She came to me for advice. Should she ask for a few thousand dollars more a year? I advised her to aim higher: ask for 10 000 more a year.

I gave this suggestion for a few reasons. One, the dollar amount she was seeking was so small, it almost wasn't worth it for the firm to talk about. It would be a lot of hassle for a few thousand dollars. Two, she actually wanted more money but was afraid it would seem greedy or demanding to name a higher figure. Like Emily, she was worried that asking for more would reflect negatively on her. And finally, usually in a negotiation, you wind up meeting somewhere in the middle. In most corporate situations, and even in start-ups, there is generally a compromise. That's the process of negotiation. You ask for a little more than you expect.

Davida also spoke to two other people, both older men she admired, and got what I considered to be the wrong advice in this situation. One, a professor of political ethics and social justice, felt that asking for more money in general was greedy. The other suggested she tell them she wanted more, but that she would take the job anyway.

I suggested, instead, that she negotiate for what she wanted. She had some leverage. They had seen her work and knew they wanted her, and she had a competing offer. I suggested she focus her conversation on the competing offer.

She was really uncomfortable stating a specific amount, but she agreed to try asking for more in general.

The conversation went very well. The head of HR praised her for asking, saying she was delighted that Davida had advocated for herself because so few women negotiate for what they want. This same HR manager also told her, unfortunately, that they probably couldn't increase her overall compensation package, given the fact that they were a tiny start-up. But they could perhaps change the mix of cash and shares (equity) in the business, giving her more cash and less equity. Davida was delighted with this outcome.

Then, they called her back. 'I spoke too soon! It went way better than I thought', Davida texted me. They'd decided to give her a slightly higher salary, and let her keep the original equity offer. She took the job, moved to San Francisco, and so far is loving it.

If you're further along in your career, you've likely developed negotiation skills. But whatever stage you are in, you should always ask for what you want. If someone wants to hire you, they've determined that you have value. In exchange for that value, you should be able to ask for what you want, within reason. You may not get it, but usually, once they've decided they want you, it won't affect getting the job.

Another way to stay focused on your own objectives is to let others in on your goals as they change, something I thought I knew, but somehow forgot about a decade ago.

I wanted to get a seat as a non-executive director to learn how corporate boards function. This is hard to do, and in an incredibly circular form of logic, most boards will only take people who have already been on a board. I'd never been on a corporate board. How would I get my start?

I was bemoaning this system to my friend Alison Davis, an experienced corporate executive and author who sits on a number of boards (and is on my personal board of directors). 'Well, have you told anybody that you want to be on a board?' she asked. No, actually, now that she mentioned it, I hadn't shared my desire widely, or followed my own advice and reached out to people I knew. I had expected a board position to somehow just happen, that people would know I wanted it and come to me with offers.

After that conversation, I started telling pretty much everyone I knew about my desire to be on a board, and that I wasn't too picky about the industry. While I knew I didn't want to be on the board of a company selling tobacco or firearms, or one that was in conflict with my current firm, beyond those stipulations, I didn't particularly care which industry I advised. I wanted the experience of being on a board and contributing to corporate growth from that vantage. I also reached out to some executive search firms. Not many companies use search firms to fill board roles, but some do, so I pursued that avenue, too.

The people I spoke to at search firms were relatively discouraging. They thought my openness to a variety of industries was 'flakey', showing a lack of direction. Also, I wasn't in the C-suite at Google, they reminded me.

I refused to be discouraged. My drive and perseverance kicked in, and I decided I would not give up until I got on a board. Not long after, a woman from one of the search firms called with an offer. 'Would you consider being on the board of a company that runs funeral homes?' she asked.

Funeral homes? Sure. I had no experience in the death care industry, and would never have gone to a search firm and said, 'I am dying to be on the board of a funeral home!' (Pun intended.) Still, *my* prize was gaining board experience, and this would give me a start.

I interviewed for, and was offered, the role. After getting permission from my employer, I accepted the position. I learned a lot about being on boards and about a field that was new to me, was able to contribute thanks to my digital background, and was on my way to other board opportunities.

Power Perspective #2: Make sure your success gets seen within your firm and beyond

You work hard. You succeed at your projects and goals. But that doesn't mean those above you always know what you've accomplished. It's your job to let them know, and to overcome any (unhelpful) qualms about seeming self-serving or full of yourself.

As much as we'd like to believe that our efforts speak for themselves, in reality, other people are busy and can easily miss your good work and/or forget to share it for you when they hear about it. A sponsor can definitely help (chapter 3), but not everyone has advocates at all times. You need to master the art of sharing your success — and doing so in a way that doesn't sound boastful or alienate colleagues.

You need to master the art of sharing your success.

Getting your success seen is important throughout your career, within your current firm and beyond it. Your career is more than your current job. You may quit this position. You may move overseas. You may change industries (see chapter 5). But your career *as a partner* will be with you for decades. Part of having a good relationship with it is keeping this broad, long-range view in mind, and protecting and building your good reputation within a broader career network.

One of the easiest ways to share your good news gracefully is to do so while highlighting the success of others, including your colleagues and your employees, if you have them. People like to be noticed and acknowledged. If you make a habit of thanking others for their good work, it's easy to include news of your success in a way that is natural and genuine.

I recently read a great example of this in a LinkedIn post by Jason Pellegrino.

Sharing your success by including others

Jason Pellegrino is the managing director and CEO of Domain Group, a New South Wales-based media and consumer-support company focused on the property market in Australia. He's a collaborative, soft-spoken, likeable guy originally from Wollongong. Here's part of Jason's post, shared after the pandemic hit the real estate market hard.

> *It has been an intense, but extraordinarily rewarding 3 years for me at Domain. We've seen two of the toughest years our property market has ever seen, punctuated by periods of amazing strength. At the same time, we've accelerated the transformation of our business from a Property Classifieds portal to an integrated Property Marketplace.*
>
> *While I often find it difficult to find the time to pause and reflect, it's a lovely feeling to be ranked #2 in Marketmeter's Australia's Best CEO's survey in the ASX100-200 in 2021.*

> ***It's a team sport. I've had the fortune of working with an amazing team across Domain who make me look good. In particular, Jolanta Masojada and Rob Doyle do so much work to help communicate Domain's strategy to our investors and engender trust. In fact, Rob himself was recognized as the #2 CFO in Marketmeter's best CFO survey in 2021 for ASX 100-200.[3]***
>
> Notice how much he has told us about himself without coming across sounding obnoxious: while real estate as a whole took a hit, he led the transformation of his company (showing his resilience and leadership), as evidenced, in part, by being ranked number two in a survey that *happens to be about the best CEOs*. He's the CEO, so this ranking is largely about him.
>
> He also used first-person plural throughout – 'we' did this and 'we' did that – which gives credit to the team, and is a gracious thing to do. And he praised others by name, making them more inclined to share this post within their own network. Finally, he shared an emotion ('It's a lovely feeling'), which helped humanise him and engender more good will toward him (rather than resentment at his success, which people can sometimes feel).
>
> All of this allowed him to let people in his wider circle know that he's just been named one of the top two CEOs in Australia, without sounding boastful.

LinkedIn can be a valuable tool for sharing your success and building your brand beyond your current job, but social media is not the only method (nor does everyone want to spend hours of their downtime online, even those who work in tech). Speaking is a great way to raise your visibility. You can volunteer to talk at local high schools and universities, at your own high school or college, on career-focused radio shows, and on industry panels and at recruiting fairs. You can offer to write for industry newsletters and blogs. Don't wait to be asked; put yourself forward. Even attending networking conferences is a way to let people beyond your current firm know what you're doing, and raise your visibility more generally.

Another, perhaps surprising, way to broaden your reputation is to throw your energy into a charity or non-profit you love. Contributing in this way can add so much to your life and might be a key part of having a great relationship with your career. Success in a non-employment arena can also help you get noticed professionally, as veteran corporate leader Cindy Carpenter has seen.

Getting known for giving back

After a long and successful career in the corporate world, Cindy Carpenter co-founded the successful consulting firm Cast. Outside of work, she was growing increasingly troubled by the plight of refugees seeking asylum in Australia. She started joining marches and donating to this cause, and then the founders of the Bread & Butter Project asked her to be chairperson of their board.

The Bread & Butter Project is a non-profit social enterprise, launched by the founders of Bourke Street Bakery, that dedicates 100 per cent of profits to providing refugees training and employment pathways in the baking and hospitality industry in Australia. Despite being busy with her job and family, Cindy agreed to chair the board. 'I couldn't say no, as the founders had been so generous and effective in their support of refugees', she says.[4]

Through her chair position, Cindy learned more about the challenges for refugees in securing employment and the valuable role of social enterprises, and began speaking as an advocate for these causes and advising other refugee-related social enterprises. This work has taken up a lot of time and emotional energy, but Cindy says the reward, 'has massively overwhelmed the hours involved'. She describes herself as gaining an enriched world view and 'soul fulfilment' from this involvement.

Recently, she and her husband invited a group of refugees from Myanmar, Afghanistan and Iran to spend the day at a small farm they own outside Sydney. None of these guests had been to the Australian countryside or swum in a dam, and many did not know how to swim at all. Paddling and eventually jumping into the water was a first for them, and very gratifying for Cindy and her family.

The weekend event also brought some 'firsts' for Cindy and her family. The visitors 'brought meat skewers taller than them to make delicious shish kebabs, flat bread a metre wide, huge platters of nuts and fruit, and music they enjoyed. They danced their hearts out, as did we', Cindy says. 'It was enormous fun.'

On the career side, Cindy has gotten a huge amount of media attention and praise for her role as chair of the board of the Bread & Butter Project. This visibility has generated new clients for Cast, including a large corporation that recently reached out with a gig focused on investing in social enterprise.

Cindy did not throw herself into this cause for attention or for business success, and yet, it has 'paid' her many times over in personal fulfilment, while also bolstering her reputation more broadly. She is known for helping make the Bread & Butter Project an enormous success, even more so than for her illustrious career. 'I've been rewarded a hundred times over by focusing on where I can be of benefit on the planet', she says.

It can definitely be hard to find time to do volunteer work, and you can't volunteer your time just for the sake of your image, or you'll burn out. You have to really care about the cause. But as Cindy's involvement with Bread & Butter shows, and Marla Stone's volunteer work with the ACLU of Southern California (chapter 2), your career and your life are on the same team, and your reputation can benefit from interests outside your job.

Power Perspective #3: Fight back (skilfully) when wronged

Another important part of maintaining a healthy career relationship is fighting back when you need to. You can rightfully expect people to treat you with respect in the workplace, regardless of your age, race, gender, background – or even performance. Even if you mess up, there are limits on how others can speak to you at work.

Fighting back does not necessarily mean waging a legal battle or even keeping a job from which you've been laid off unfairly. But it does mean finding a way to feel good about your career and your agency overall. It might mean speaking up for yourself, then moving on.

Most companies have HR departments to protect people from harassment and to manage the employee experience. There is a global conversation around bullying and harassment happening now, and these situations are incredibly varied, upsetting and tricky. I don't have the legal or psychological expertise to offer advice on these really tough scenarios, but if it happens to you, definitely reach out to someone who does. Even in less egregious situations, if you're on the receiving end of unethical or unfair behaviour, you should report it.

Fighting back can take stamina, and it can feel risky when you need to earn a living. But it also builds stamina because it helps you not over-focus on the negative or take setbacks personally. It's a way of asserting your rights and protecting your positive view of yourself. There are definitely times when you shouldn't fight back, such as when you are in the wrong. But in general, standing up for yourself helps ensure that you can walk away from a negative experience with a positive view of yourself in your career intact.

It's a way of asserting your rights and protecting your positive view of yourself.

As Margie Warrell, an inspirational author, coach and podcaster with a PhD in Human and Organizational Development, puts it:

> ***If you tolerate someone overstepping your boundaries, making snide remarks or overlooking you for opportunities, you can generally expect more of the same. By not making a very clear stand for what you will, and will not, tolerate, you become complicit in your own misery.***[5]

Standing up for yourself by upholding good boundaries can mean removing yourself from a toxic work environment, and getting into a better one. Take the case of a man I'll call Bo, who started his career in a training program at a global firm. He worked his way up through the ranks, got promoted several times, and was asked to move to a new country. He was doing really well.

He'd been with the company for about eight years, when a new person was appointed to run his team, a woman who had been working in another division. Bo had heard she was difficult, but he really liked his job and thought he should give her the benefit of the doubt.

Unfortunately, almost as soon as this new manager took over, she started making demeaning comments about people in the group. She even shouted at individuals during meetings. A number of times, in public settings, she loudly criticised Bo, someone who had always been a strong performer. In virtual meetings with Bo, she would yell at him so loudly that people who were working in the office with her elsewhere on the floor would message Bo to ask if he was alright.

Despite asking for feedback, Bo was unable to determine concrete actions he could take to deliver what the new boss seemed to want. Most strikingly, none of Bo's advocates, who were themselves reasonably senior, felt comfortable taking on this woman.

It was clear to Bo that this unhealthy environment was unlikely to change. Ultimately, it spurred him to finally look for a job in fintech, something he'd been thinking about for a while. He took time to look for a role he really liked, and that would provide comparable pay. Bo is now happy at a high-growth payments company. Bo did the right thing by looking after his wellbeing and his career by extricating himself from a terrible work situation, but leveraging his experience and contacts to further his professional goals.

Ideally, your sponsors and board of directors will help you strategise, as they did in the case of a young engineer who I'll call Kathy, who had a bad boss at her first real job.

Confronting demoralising jerkiness

Kathy landed a role in the product department of a large, multinational firm where she had interned for two summers. She was excited to have a role there, but her manager quickly became a problem. He told her repeatedly that she wasn't doing a good job and that she was 'just not promotable'. Kathy asked for specific feedback to help her improve. Instead of providing direction, her boss started leaving her out of projects, ignoring her and decreasing the frequency of their meetings.

The situation was growing more and more stressful. She was being told she was doing a bad job, yet had no way to improve. She finally went to HR and said that she wanted to be successful and didn't understand her boss's treatment of her. HR advised her boss to offer her constructive feedback. Instead, he went to the old Google doc of their past meetings and filled it in retrospectively with fake complaints, things he'd never told her and that were not addressable. It seemed like he was building a case against her rather than trying to help her develop.

She felt so demoralised and undervalued that, after a while, it started affecting her health. She really liked the firm, but her position was untenable. She reached out to an advocate she had in a different division, someone senior for whom she'd interned, who knew her to be a great contributor. He suggested she try to get transferred internally, rather than leave the company altogether.

She reached out to me for advice, and I agreed that she needn't leave the firm, necessarily. She was worried that her boss had damaged her image irrevocably within the firm. I assured her that the company was more than large enough for her to stay on, and avoid him. She had a good track record there. I didn't think she should sacrifice the positive reputation and strong foundation she had built there in order to avoid one guy – who might leave one day.

She decided to try. She then did something that I thought was appropriate but very brave, especially for a young woman in a large firm. She reached out to the chief product officer (CPO), a man several levels above her boss who she'd met once or twice, and with whom she shared an outside interest. She told him about her situation with her boss, that she was looking to move internally, and that she wondered if there might be a role within his division. It's scary to go over the head of an immediate boss, damaging to that relationship and often inappropriate, but in this case, her connection with her boss was irrevocably frayed, and the HR department wasn't helping. Her choices were to do whatever she could to transfer – or leave. In other words, she had nothing left to lose.

She was also emboldened to reach out to the CPO because she knew that a young female engineer had just quit, and management was worried that a toxic environment might be the cause. In the current environment, it's a big deal for a firm to lose an engineer; there's never enough tech talent, and female engineers are extra rare.

A couple days later, she got a call about a role in a different division, due to the CPO asking around and advocating for her. She also found a second option at a subsidiary of the same multinational. She created a good outcome from a bad situation by standing up for herself and moving on to something better.

Sometimes a firm really is acting illegally or unethically. It can take nerve and support to fight back. Doing so may not mean staying at the firm, but rather figuring out exactly what you want the firm to do for you and asking for it, as a woman, who I'll call Li Ling, working in Singapore, did.

Go down fighting to keep your career relationship strong

I was taking a walk behind my house on a path through Singapore's rainforest, multitasking as usual – in this case, mentoring Li Ling by phone while getting some exercise. It was late afternoon, not too hot for Singapore, though I was sweaty from walking. Over the sound of birdcalls and traffic, Li Ling told me what happened.

(*continued*)

About a month earlier, she'd been celebrated for being the top sales performer in Asia within her company, a California-based tech firm with an office in Singapore. Two weeks after the firm announced her success internally, she told her boss that she was pregnant. Two weeks after that, she was fired. This was at the beginning of the COVID lockdown in Singapore. Sales were down, and the company had been laying off weak performers, Li Ling said. But the top sales performer who just happened to be pregnant? The pregnancy and termination looked undeniably linked.

She knew she needed to do something, but what? What they had done was wrong, and she wanted to fight back in some way.

Pregnancy discrimination laws in California ban employers from using pregnancy as a 'motivating reason' to terminate you. But Li Ling was based in Singapore and hired through one of the professional employer organisation companies that firms often use when they are first establishing offices in a new country. The US tech firm had assured her that she was truly part of the team, but then backtracked on that rhetoric when it really mattered. I'd seen other Silicon Valley firms dismiss women working outside headquarters in similarly unfair or questionable ways.

'What do you really want to happen?' I asked.

She thought about it. She didn't really want to stay at the firm; the thought that they'd felt entitled to fire her for being pregnant had ruined the culture for her.

She wanted a better severance package, she realised, and health insurance to cover her pregnancy and the months after birth.

I advised her to write a letter making this request, and to speak to a lawyer, so she'd know her rights. The conversation with the lawyer helped give her courage to write the letter because she learned that the firm might be seen as violating Singapore's maternity leave protections. Her letter was polite and professional, but it laid out the facts and her suspicion of the company's wrongdoing: she was hired through a separate firm but was clearly told that she was part of the main firm; she'd recently gotten a 17 per cent salary raise, been the top performing sales director, built up a team of 20 people and generated a couple million in revenue; the other people laid off in her department were junior, and one retained was on probation. 'As I am the only pregnant person on the team, it appears to me to be the only plausible reason for my selection', she wrote.

She explained that the severance package the company had offered did not reflect her accomplishments or the practice of other Silicon Valley firms, and that she wanted something more appropriate. She suggested some options, including that the firm retain her for six more months, or let her go now but pay her full salary for a year and her medical insurance until several months after the birth of her child.

She ended her letter on a positive note (that included a bit of dig at the firm's blatant hypocrisy):

> *I am so proud of having given my all over the past 2 + years and having been part of a firm that won 'best company culture' awards. I would like to leave knowing that, even though the economic situation is presenting challenges, [the firm] still has the culture which drew me to it in the first place.*

This wrap-up mattered. Reiterating her accomplishments and documenting them in writing helped preserve and present her positive narrative of her career. She'd been a very successful leader at a reputable firm, and this was the vision of herself she would be taking forward.

It was a strong letter. Still, she was worried about hitting 'send', and concerned people in the firm might bad mouth her to others, hurting her prospects elsewhere. This would have been unlikely, given the company's interest in maintaining its good reputation and not wanting to disclose the details of her termination.

She sent the letter. The result? She left the firm with a good feeling about herself and a much better severance deal, one with more money and the postnatal healthcare coverage she needed.

She went on to have her baby and get a great new job with a different start-up.

Fighting back can also mean not accepting someone else's assessment of a sticky situation. I know of an Italian woman who moved to Asia with her husband and then accepted a role with an American multinational corporation. Once there, she found herself falling for a man at work, someone with more seniority, though not her direct boss.

They began an affair. She separated from her spouse, and believed it when her senior co-worker said he would do the same. But he changed his mind.

She should quit, he told her. They couldn't work together any longer, and he had a family to support. At first, this young woman took his view of the situation as fact. She went to her boss to resign, sharing with him what had happened. She didn't have another job lined up or any other source of income, and she no longer had a spouse to help weather the transition.

Her boss asked if she really wanted to resign, but didn't push back against her decision. I find his behaviour wholly inexplicable. He should have stuck up for his employee and investigated a little, rather than assuming that, of course, the woman and the person with less power should be the one to lose her job.

After thinking it over, she decided she didn't want to resign. She went back to her boss and asked for a role in a different part of the firm. This was a huge company, and her boss was able to find her another position. I was glad to hear that she took some time to think about what she wanted in her career and advocated for herself.

Be the change

One way to improve the culture at work for yourself and for those coming after you is to advocate for change. Advocating does not have to be adversarial. In my case, and in the case of many women of my generation, just persisting has been a form of advocating – being the first woman in a position in an industry or the first woman leader. You become a role model and a change agent merely by showing up and doing a good job.

You also help create change by bringing a different perspective to the conversation as a result of your experiences. Debra Haaland, the New Mexico congresswoman who became the first Native American cabinet secretary in US history in 2021, referenced this type of advocacy when running for the House of Representatives. She campaigned under the slogan: 'Congress has never heard a voice like mine.'[6]

Advocating can also mean getting clear about what you want, and asking for it, even if it seems extreme by the current standards at your place of work. Piruze sees herself as helping establish new norms at the company, not only for herself, but also for parents coming after her. She is working with her boss to create a '100-day Back-to-Work Plan' for new parents. 'That's how we will change things', she says. 'They brought me in for a fresh perspective. I feel like I'm not doing my job well if I don't try.'

Another way of advocating for change is pushing for more flexibility at work. One way to achieve this is through a type of job sharing that is already the norm in a number of professions, such as veterinarian medicine and pharmacy, a fact pointed out by economic historian Claudia Goldin, author of *Career and Family: Women's Century-Long Journey Toward Equity*. If your dog is sick late at night, your veterinarian doesn't leave the dinner table to come see him; you go to an emergency clinic. Similarly, when you call in a prescription, any number of different pharmacists could fill it. Even OB/GYNs show up for each other to deliver babies.

'I'm amazed when a lawyer, accountant, consultant or financier makes a case for non substitutability among professionals in his area, but can't answer why delivering a baby isn't the equivalent', Goldin writes.[7]

I certainly see other evidence that attitudes are changing. A Dutch woman I know who runs a sales team and whose husband stays home with their two kids recently told me that her seven-year-old daughter raised the topic of marriage. My friend said to her daughter, 'You know, you don't have to get married'. To which her daughter responded, 'But if I don't get married, who will look after the kids?'

Power Perspective #4: Set boundaries

Not only do you have a right to be treated respectfully at work, but you also have other rights that might need to be protected, such as the freedom to disconnect from work and work-related technology at the end of the day and on weekends. You have a right to get enough sleep and spend time with family and friends. Setting boundaries is a way of preserving these very important rights, and as such, part of having a healthy relationship with your career.

One important boundary to set is around email and other electronic messaging. Technology can lead to the assumption that employees should be reachable at all times. This belief or expectation translates into *never* having a break from work, which compromises productivity and happiness, as many of us saw during the pandemic. The technology-driven, 24-hour workday is such a problem for employees and firms that some countries have enacted laws and/or guidelines to grant workers the 'right to disconnect'. These include things like setting time limits around when employees must answer company emails or phone calls, and a prohibition against penalising those who don't respond to requests outside of working hours.

France, Italy and Spain have all legislated to different degrees the right to log off after working hours. In Germany, employees can negotiate with companies for this right. Ireland has adopted a code of practice to digitally disconnect that includes remote workers and people working from home. The EU, recognising the problem of the 'always on' culture, is looking into establishing a directive for member countries.[8]

These are important developments that should help people maintain good career relationships by keeping work in check. In my own life as the head of APAC for US-based companies, I had to learn to set boundaries to prevent work from overtaking everything else. It was absolutely necessary for all of us in Singapore to take this issue seriously to keep our sanity and prevent our days from feeling like 'time soup'. I realised, for example, that I could only do midnight or dawn meetings twice a week if I had any hope of being a fully functional human being. I had to establish clear boundaries around meetings and communicate them to headquarters and model them for my team.

It's normal in an overseas office for the workday to stretch long into the night or start super early to accommodate the time zone of those in headquarters or team members in other parts of the world. But wherever you work, when parts of your job must be done outside of normal office hours, you should allocate time in the day for your personal life in return. If I have a late-night meeting, I take time to exercise or handle other personal tasks between nine and five. I learned to set boundaries with carve-outs for personal time. This is an increasingly important skill today, as so many offices are going virtual or hybrid, and many people work with global teams.

Another kind of boundary may sound surprising – setting a boundary around the ways in which you'll be helpful to the team or to clients. You don't want to create work for yourself that is completely outside your role, as a young woman I mentored learned after she'd been working for a while.

Being of service but not subservient

A young woman I know transferred to a small, new office of her firm as a junior executive. The office itself was not yet set up. The company had allocated money for it, but no one was really available to do the work right away. This woman's brother came to visit on vacation, and the two of them went to IKEA and bought shelves and furniture for the office, then put everything together themselves. She also ordered the snacks for the office.

She was doing all this administrative work, and other people noticed, and commented on how nice it was of her to make the office comfortable.

It was nice of her, and nice *for them*, but not ultimately a good move for her career or aspirations to be a leader.

I reminded her, 'You are not the office manager. This is not your job. Doing it is creating a role for yourself that you shouldn't have.'

(*continued*)

Yes, you want to be helpful and a team player, but there is a difference between helping in a way that supports your career, and in a way that doesn't.

She was surprised by this feedback. As she said later, 'It was a big shift for me to understand that if I want to be respected as an executive I should make sure I'm equal in all ways.'[9]

Later, I went to a client meeting with this same woman where she made an effort to arrive early with bagels and coffee and offered to take notes. It was *nice*, but not necessary, and maybe not beneficial to her goals.

Again, this was a mindshift for my young colleague.

> ***In my first job, the team was all women. Everyone would bring bagels and coffee. It wasn't negative, but thinking about it later, I wondered if the customers considered me more as an office manager than as an executive in the room. Did they align me in their minds more with their daughter or wife than with their colleagues? I think they may have. Also, would they have been just as likely to serve the coffee to me? I'm always going to be of service, but I realized that it's not a good idea to be seen as subservient.***

It's a common pattern; the women in the office take on the helper's role. It is almost always the women who bring donuts or volunteer to clean up after a meeting. If she had been going out of her way to help other people close deals, that would have been a great way to be of service. The company would likely notice, and she'd be setting herself up to ask for a leadership role in sales. But that's different to over-contributing on getting snacks.

People often expect women to do these things, but why should they? Plenty of guys are considered nice, and no one expects them to get out an Allen wrench to build the office shelves themselves or bring the coffee.

As a leader, you should model good boundary-setting for others around, not only your activities, but also your time. I always kept my online calendar accessible to let team members see how I was spending my time, including my daily 60-minute gym visit. This communicates the idea that personal time is valued in the office, and others should make time for it, too.

Piruze (from chapter 1) decided that she would enlist others in her efforts to keep and model good boundaries after returning to work from her second maternity leave. She set personal boundaries around phone calls, asking her assistant not to schedule calls between 6 pm and 8.30 pm, when she would be putting her kids to sleep. (If needed, she would take calls after 8.30 pm.)

As a leader, you should model good boundary-setting for others.

She knew this would be a hard boundary for her to keep, particularly because she was in a high-visibility role, so she shared this goal with others beyond her assistant, and asked for their support.

> ***Even without an assistant, I think you can be vulnerable and ask for help. You can talk to the people closest to you about what's important to you, share with your partner and colleagues that setting boundaries is something hard for you and make sure they help. It's like how if you're on a diet and love sugar, you can avoid sugary things by not having them around the house.***

As Piruze points out, setting and holding boundaries is another one of those work skills that can improve with time.

> ***We grow in our jobs. We get feedback. We reflect. It's continuous learning. I wasn't always so good at holding these kinds of boundaries in the past, but I think I am learning my lessons and will be able to do it better now.***

Takeaways

- You are in a relationship with your career. It's your job to develop the best relationship you can over the years.
- Even a great career can't fulfil all your needs. Don't damage your career relationship by having unrealistic expectations of what a job can or 'should' do for you.
- Keep your eye on your prize — as in, recognise and pursue your goals. Don't wait around for someone else to notice your good work or hand you the promotion or opportunity you want. You have to identify your desires and go for them.
- Make sure your success gets seen. Practice the art of self-promotion with style.
- Fight back when wronged. Standing up for yourself can be hard to do, but it's part of maintaining a good relationship with your career.
- Set boundaries around work and personal life to get the most from both.

mindshift five

Get a move on! Use movement to stay energised and thrive

Power perspectives in this chapter

- prepare for your promotion
- be flexible and persistent
- make one move at a time
- create momentum where you are.

Lisa Wang, a 30-something Chinese-American from California, has had a somewhat nonlinear career path, moving from job to job and location to location. 'I changed all sorts of functions and jobs and worked in big and small companies. I was prioritising gaining new experiences that were fulfilling to me as an individual', she says.[1]

As she got older, she began to worry about all this movement. Was it really so wise? 'I would see other people who I had worked with previously, who had more direct paths, and they seemed to get promoted faster.'

In her late twenties, still prioritising adventure over acceleration, she moved to Asia. This move meant putting aside an interest she had in product management because most of the opportunities in Asia were in sales. She worked for me in Singapore (and was befriended by another young woman from San Francisco, Emily Huo, from chapter 1).

After working in sales operations in Asia for a few years, Lisa returned to the US to pursue an MBA at Harvard University. She graduated, took a job – and then quickly left it when she realised it wasn't for her.

Suddenly, faced with a break in employment, she stopped to think about her direction. She'd done so many things, yet never focused on moving toward her long-standing interest in product management. Was it too late to make that switch? 'Product management is pretty competitive and people like to hire employees with demonstrated experience. I thought: *Let me just try. It could be my last chance.*'

She had some interviews, but struck out repeatedly. She'd been working as a team leader at huge, multinational firms, and had great experience and education, yet even when applying for an individual contributor role in product development at Instagram – a role without management responsibility – she was rejected. 'I'm generally a person who is good at interviewing. I could tell this was indicative of a bigger problem in terms of my experience', she says.

Lisa sought advice from product managers who'd had nonlinear careers to learn how they'd made the transition. She came to an important conclusion: she'd have to target smaller companies with looser requirements for the role in order to switch from sales to product.

Taking this approach, after four months of looking, she finally landed a role as the first product management hire at a San Francisco–based start-up with about 70 employees. Because of its small size, the company was willing to take a chance on someone without direct experience in product management. It also meant that she was thrown into all kinds of meetings and business areas that she would never have been exposed to at a larger firm.

During the pandemic, the start-up faltered. Lisa once again found herself looking for a product management job. This time, however, she had experience. A product marketing lead for monetisation opened at Instagram, a more senior role than the one she'd pursued a year earlier. This time, she applied, and got the position.

Lisa is still at Instagram, and she loves it. She credits her success there, in part, to all that movement.

> ***I think about things more holistically now, and look at things in different ways. If you prioritise exploration, it can make you more successful because you bring a different point of view, insights that are often lacking. It makes you a well-rounded professional with a broader perspective. All of these things in your career accumulate, the people you meet, the experiences you have, and the skills you develop. Things have a crazy way of working out.***

The 'Ah-ha!' of Lisa's story: movement can maximise your value

While there used to be a stigma associated with job hopping – a notion that it implied a lack of loyalty or stick-to-it-iveness – today, it is often part of rising and thriving. We evolve, and so should our careers – at the beginning, 10 years in, even 20 years in. (I switched almost 30 years in!) Careers are long, and you have time to try different jobs, firms, industries and sectors.

Even heading down what ultimately turns out to be a road to nowhere doesn't have the negative impact it once might have. As Lisa Wang says:

> ***At Instagram, when we evaluate business decisions, we ask, 'Is this a one-way door?' If it is, you have to very carefully evaluate whether you're willing to cut off all other paths. But the truth is, in your career, there are very few one-way doors. There are very few decisions you can't come back from.***

Trying different jobs, fields, industries and sectors is not only common today but also increasingly beneficial for you – and for the firms that employ you. While it is important to stay in a position long enough to gain from it and do well at it, in general, you're going to need a broad range of experiences and perspectives to rise. Moving around is how you gain them. A blog post on the Australian Institute of Business's (AIB) site describes the benefits of new opportunities this way:

> ***It affords you a chance to build up a wider network of professional contacts and exposes you to different functions, workplace cultures and management styles, which will stand you in good stead for when you move up the ranks yourself.***[2]

Even people who got their start when long-term loyalty to a firm was prized switch firms more frequently today than in the past. According to the AIB, in Australia, employees today change jobs 12 times throughout their lives, on average, with people over the age of 45 staying in one position for less than seven years, and those under 25 moving on after less than two years.[3]

In the US, the median tenure of workers between the ages of 55 and 64 is just about 10 years. While for those aged 25–34 it was just under three years.[4] As Chris Kolmar, an internet marketer and co-founder of Zippia, a US-based career advice and job listings platform, puts it, '91% of Millennials expect to change jobs every three years.[5]

One reason that movement has become part of rising and thriving is that our increasing longevity means careers last far longer than they used to. Most people will have more than a few jobs in their lives, and perhaps even different careers. 'As lives lengthen, at least two new decades have been gifted to humans and their working lives', says Avivah Wittenberg-Cox, CEO of 20-first, a global consultancy focused on helping firms achieve gender balance and create intergenerational teams.[6] You might work for 30 years in one profession, then work another 20 in something else. Movement helps maintain stamina for the long haul. As Wittenberg-Cox says, '... increasingly fit and active fifty-year olds are discovering they may have several more decades of working life ahead'. My own moves have kept me energised and excited about work throughout my career, and about the new challenges in my current stage: Aliza 3.0.

Another reason movement has become more common is that the velocity of change has accelerated in general, and this is true in jobs as well. New opportunities and entirely new fields arise with record speed.

Many of today's roles didn't exist a decade ago. I could not have planned to work for Google when I graduated from college because it didn't exist. Likewise, some great careers of the future probably aren't around yet. Meanwhile, other industries have contracted and positions have disappeared entirely, rendering some skill sets obsolete and requiring practitioners to retrain to stay employed.

Moving geographically can be a great way to get more responsibility sooner. The increasingly global nature of work makes moving overseas with your firm or profession far more doable than in the past, and more advantageous for you and your firm. (See chapter 6 for tips on working overseas.)

Options for movement are influenced by a variety of factors; during the pandemic, international relocation became much harder, if not impossible in some cases. Then, as countries reopened after long lockdowns, dramatic changes in the world of work made it one of the best times to seek a new role or to push for benefits. As employers scrambled to fill vacancies, employees had far more leverage than previously. With people having had the experience of working from home, many firms were far more open to a hybrid work style and flexible hours.

In general, aim to leave your current job when there is something you want to go *toward*, rather than waiting until you want to flee where you are. You want to bring an open, adventurous attitude to vetting opportunities, rather than waiting until you're demoralised, and grabbing the first thing that comes along. I'm not suggesting you should pursue a new position when you *love* your current one, but ideally, you'll move on when you see something else you really like, even if your current job is more or less fine.

Sometimes you have to leave a job before you have a specific destination in mind – because it's become too bad to stay, for personal reasons, or because your position is eliminated. If you wind up moving when angry or really bored, try to bring an open, interested mindset to your job search.

You can change your mind about what you want to do for your day job, which sector or field you want to be part of, and even where in the world you want to work. As with everything else in your career, if you want to make a move – whether it's up or sideways or even down temporarily – you need to take charge of how it unfolds. Here's how.

Power Perspective #1: Prepare for your promotion

The most common direction people think about when it comes to career movement is *up*, as in a promotion. Not everyone aims to rise from their current position, of course, and many people specifically don't want a life of constantly chasing the next big title or raise. As Simon Kantor (from chapter 1) says:

> ***We spend so much of our life looking up and saying, 'When am I going to have that?' And so little of our life looking sideways and saying, 'It's quite nice here. And maybe this is alright.'*[7]**

I think gratitude for what you have is very important. Sometimes you might even take a step back as part of moving forward. But if you are looking to move up within your organisation, there's one rule I always encourage people to follow: prepare for your promotion first, *then* ask for it.

Another way to think about this: 'de-risk' your promotion for your boss by demonstrating that you can do the work. Even if it's clear to *you* that you're ready, it may not be so obvious to those above you. Also, others are probably angling for the job or title. Organisational life can be very competitive. Very often, there simply aren't enough top jobs to go around. Even within a huge global corporation, there may be only one senior position that's right for you at any given time – and a handful of other people eager to land it. Collaborating well, working hard and even having good outcomes may not be enough.

You need to prove you can do the job you are angling for.

Promotions are nuanced, and the route to rising is not totally linear or transparent. Most businesses haven't established exact criteria; you generally don't get a handout with three specific steps to take to prepare for your promotion. Even within a company that has a framework for skills needed at each level, the assessment of these skills is not an exact science, and other factors are in play. The ambiguity around getting promoted is one reason people can feel frustrated in the business world and another example of how it is very different to university; you can't just do A-level work and be guaranteed to rise.

Often, you need to prove you can do the job you are angling for.

Many managers encourage this approach overtly. They'll say, 'We want to see that you're already doing the job before we officially give you the role'. Ideally, your manager will also help you figure out how to rise and find opportunities to demonstrate your readiness. A woman I know worked at a firm that had an internal framework for promotion, a list of a dozen attributes people needed to show to move up. She was doing a great job on some, operating above her current level in the customer-centric part of her job. But as her boss pointed out, no one had seen her demonstrate other attributes, such as thinking globally and being strategic when establishing direction for the group or company. Her boss did what a good boss should do; he sought opportunities for her to practice these skills and demonstrate them. He found other managers who had upcoming projects she could work on to develop these attributes, and he invited her to help him develop the strategic plan for the following year.

Throughout my career, I've helped employees think through what they want to do next, and what they need to do to show progress toward their goals. A manager should do this, but if you aren't getting that support, take charge of planning yourself.

Start by really thinking about what you want to do next, and create a work plan to get there. Find ways to assume some of the responsibilities you'd like to take on at the next level. See if you can manage one or two people, for example, to gain demonstrable leadership experience. Take on a project involving higher-level analytics. Volunteer to help out if a new role arises. If you have a good relationship with your boss, ask to meet to talk through your goals and strategise ways to achieve them. It's much better to get buy-in and support, if you can, than to go it alone. After six or 12 months of doing the work for the next role, and succeeding at it, you have real evidence to show when you ask for a promotion.

Sometimes there just isn't a promotion available in your office or region. Ideally, your boss will tell you this candidly, though it can be hard for a manager to admit to a good employee that there is no room for advancement. If your boss does share this reality, you can ask for details, but then you have to accept the truth. As one leader I've mentored told me, 'Sometimes I tell people that the company isn't investing in leaders at that level in this office, and they fight it, instead of listening'. If you want to rise and thrive, and there's no opportunity where you are, you have to take action, as in move to another part of the business or to another firm.

Or you can wait, in some cases, but you may be waiting a long time. I know a guy who was next in line to be country head at his firm, but the person who had that job wasn't leaving. There was one role, and it was filled. He had two choices: he could go somewhere else or he could wait. He waited for five years, and finally got the role. This kind of limitation is more likely in a small market, a small company, or a specialised division within a huge firm, like the legal department in a tech firm that may have only one general counsel role.

Help your employees rise

If you are a leader, it is your job to help your employees develop and to get deserving ones promoted. Period. You recruit, retain and develop talent for your firm. Being involved in their trajectory and supporting it is part of doing your job. It also helps increase their engagement at work and commitment to the firm. You help employees rise in a few very specific ways:

- **Highlight their strengths.** Tell them what they are good at and give examples of times they have used valuable strengths. People grow by recognising and building on strengths. It also boosts morale and confidence, which helps people rise.
- **Provide constructive feedback.** If certain skills are missing or not visible, provide clear feedback on what they need to show or where they should improve.

- **Create development opportunities.** Not only should you let them know what to focus on but you should also help them come up with opportunities to develop those skills.
- **Manage expectations.** It's your job to let your employees know when a promotion is likely to occur, or isn't. There may not be a need for a higher-level person in your country or business at that moment, meaning a promotion isn't possible, even if a person is ready for it. Be honest with employees, and let them know when it isn't their fault.

Helping an engineer develop and get promoted

I once worked with a solutions engineer who was eager to advance in the firm. He knew the product incredibly well and could answer detailed questions about it. But his job also involved pre-sales consulting with potential clients. He was not excelling at this part of the job.

While he knew the product, he didn't really know how to listen to customers and think creatively about ways the product might address their concerns. If a customer asked, 'Can your product do this?' he might answer immediately, 'No'. This shut down the conversation and prevented the relationship from really developing.

It also wasn't necessarily true. It was entirely possible that the product could have helped the customer, if that person had posed the question differently. As a general rule in sales, you never reply to a client's question brusquely with a one syllable 'no'. You shouldn't lie, but you should ask questions to get a better understanding of their needs, a skill this engineer needed to develop.

As his managers started coaching him to take on more responsibility, they emphasised this very specific, learnable skill.

(*continued*)

He needed to ask open-ended questions, such as, 'What is the issue you're trying to solve?' And, 'Why do you want this specific thing?' With a clearer understanding of the customer's goal, he could figure out if the product could help with that aim in some way.

By receiving feedback over and over after each customer meeting, he developed this skill that he needed to rise.

This was a particularly good situation because what he needed to learn was very clear, and he was quite open to feedback and very coachable. He got a promotion and began managing other engineers. Now, in a somewhat surprising move (considering where he started), he's left the engineering department and moved into sales.

To be or not to be (a student again)

People often wonder if they should pursue further education of some sort to help them rise in their career. You can definitely pursue formal education, a certificate or accreditation program as part of your promotion plan, whether that means a graduate degree, like the MBA I did to use the swimming pool at NYU, or shorter, skills-based courses. Some companies will pay for continuing education, and it can benefit you in numerous ways. As the AIB puts it:

> ***Not only will those extra qualifications and courses look good on your resume, they're an excellent way to demonstrate to employers that you're prepared to put in additional effort in order to deliver results... When the promotion opportunity does come along, your up-to-date knowledge and skills will put you at the front of the pack.***[8]

I support lifelong learning, and more education will never hurt you—but it won't *guarantee* you a promotion. More education is always good, and with today's accelerated pace of change, retraining and retooling your skills is often necessary. But don't get another degree strictly as a route to promotion—or rely on it as your sole strategy for rising.

Perhaps it should go without saying, but you also do need to ask to be promoted. As the AIB puts it:

> ***Many people make the mistake of deciding that they're not yet ready for a promotion and hanging back while their peers leapfrog them. It sounds obvious, but if you don't ask or apply for a promotion, it's unlikely that you'll get one. Even if you are turned down because you're not quite ready yet, it signals your ambition and willingness to learn, which can open up a conversation about what you need to demonstrate you're ready. A good leader will always support the career trajectory of their staff once they know who wants to go that extra mile.***

Because getting promoted from within is often a challenge and takes time, when accepting a new job, really pay attention to the title offered, and try to come in at as high a level as you can. A woman I know working in Australia, who I'll call Justine, is a perfect example of someone who negotiated for a higher position than she was offered—and got it, even while changing industries.

Justine wanted to transition from an operating role into being a private equity (PE) investor. She got a job offer to be a sort-of junior partner at a mid-sized private equity firm. Her would-be boss assured her that there would be opportunity to grow into a full partner role later. But Justine knew that she'd be better off entering at the level she really wanted, if she could. She countered with a suggestion that she be hired as a full partner—and she found data to support her assertion that she could do the job at that level. 'I looked at what my peers in the U.S. were doing to bring in senior women to PE and found a job description online of a partner role from a very prominent U.S.-based PE firm,' she says. 'It showed what a partner does and what kind of experience they want that person to bring.'

She shared the document with the managing partner, telling him that she felt she could do the role and had the requisite background. She also gave an impressive reference, a former boss of hers who she knew the manager admired and respected. 'It's not like you can just show a job description and say how great you are. You have to think strategically about how else you can show them that you are at their level,' she says.

Justine offered to help the firm find a junior-level employee from her own network if the job they were offering her could not be recast at a higher level. She stressed that she wanted the firm to succeed and would do what she could to help, but that she only wanted to come in as a full partner. 'I was being fair and open and not lying or playing games. I was being vulnerable but also being firm,' she says.

All of this strategising paid off. She got offered the full partner role and is very happy with it and with the firm.

Power Perspective #2: Be flexible and persistent

Of course, not all moves are directly up. Plenty of people seek to change roles, fields, firms or even sectors, and while this can be a valuable and exciting part of a rewarding career, it also may require some real flexibility. When I moved to Google from financial services in my forties, I accepted a lower title. I did this because I really wanted to learn about the Internet and had no experience in the field. Plus, I realised that tech had less 'title inflation' than financial services: equivalent-level jobs would have one title in a tech firm, and a far more prestigious-sounding title in banking.

I also took a salary cut, again because I wanted the job, and hoped that the equity (stock) portion of my package would more than compensate for the short-term salary dip, which it did over time. These accommodations were a necessary part of moving into a new field that intrigued me, and I was willing to make them, though a woman at a top global executive search firm said I was 'brave' to make this transition. I think she meant 'foolhardy', but my decision worked out well.

I haven't had a senior VP title since, but my world greatly expanded, as did my influence and impact. I've had an amazing career and gotten access to board memberships and other opportunities that might have not come my way had I stayed in financial services.

Like me, you might have an opportunity that pays less at first, or one that is structured to include more risk, either in a higher percentage of variable pay or more equity versus salary. In general, you shouldn't have to take a salary dip, particularly if you construct your narrative well and can explain how your skills transfer, but you might be faced with a situation that makes it worthwhile. Don't limit your opportunity for adventure or dampen your enthusiasm by being overly rigid, even about pay. Making a move – and thriving from it – does not necessarily mean getting a more senior title.

Making a move – and thriving from it – does not necessarily mean getting a more senior title.

A plan for advancement might require a move backward at first, even one you hadn't planned, something Sue Shilbury realised when she attempted to move into hospital management.

One step back, two steps forward

Sue, originally from Perth, worked as physiotherapist for about six years in a children's hospital. During this time, she realised that she didn't want to do hands-on work forever, and that she wanted a role with more responsibility and higher pay. All of this led her to pursue an MBA at the Australian Graduate School of Management in New South Wales, one of the country's top business programs. Her plan was to get her degree then transition into hospital management, ideally running administrative services at a children's hospital. This, she figured, would allow her to capitalise on her years of experience in physiotherapy doing hands-on patient care, while also utilising her new business education.

After graduating, she started applying for low-level hospital management positions. To her dismay, she kept getting rejected. Hiring managers said she lacked the experience needed for the role she wanted. She did get a few offers, but they paid less than her salary as a physiotherapist, back before she earned her MBA.

(*continued*)

Finally, a man in the healthcare industry offered some helpful advice. He suggested she get yet *more* education, specifically with a two-year, management development program.

This, he assured her, would fill the gap in her experience.

Sue did not want to undertake more education after just earning her MBA, but without any decent offers, she decided to take the advice and enrol at what was then called the Australian College of Health Service Management. The program allowed her to gain experience and training on the job. She worked full time at St Vincent's Hospital in Sydney as part of the two-year, on-the-job program. Within six months, someone senior left the organisation and Sue was appointed to that role. This would not have happened had she not been in the program and aware of positions as soon as they arose. She went on to rise in hospital management, landing higher-paying roles with more responsibility. Her plan to get a degree and switch directions worked; it just took a little more education than she'd expected. As she says about her experience, 'Sometimes you have to take a step back to go forward.'[9]

Another version of being flexible when trying to move is noticing when a small change might be movement enough. If you're looking for something different, it's easy to assume you need a wholesale career overhaul. But a smaller tweak might suffice, something my co-writer, Wendy, realised in 2007.

After leaving WNBC-TV in New York, she focused on freelance writing for magazines, websites and radio shows, and got a Master's Degree in Nonfiction Creative Writing from Columbia University. Over time, as technology ate into the ad structure of legacy journalism, and the economic downturn hit the industry hard, assignments for freelancers began drying up. Faced with declining revenue and a glut of experienced journalists, many places cut the per-word rate (how freelance writers were generally compensated). Wendy loved reporting and writing, meeting new people and learning new things, but she found herself wondering: *Was it time to get out of journalism?*

She took a career transition workshop offered by the alumni association of Columbia University. One new insight she gleaned: maybe the solution wasn't so black or white, quit or stay.

> ***One thing they suggested was looking for a specific aspect of your current work that you don't like and could change, rather than jumping to the conclusion that you must leave the field entirely. I realised that I loved working with magazines and doing feature journalism. What I didn't like was the instability of freelance, the uncertainty and constant pitching. I also wanted to be in more of a leadership role. All of this led me to look for a job as a magazine editor on staff rather than remaining an article writer, which was at the time almost entirely done by freelancers.***

Wendy found a listing for a senior editor at *Psychology Today* magazine, based in New York City, near where she was living at the time, and applied for the job. She got the position and left freelancing without leaving journalism behind.

Sometimes, moving to a new, great job can require yet another kind of flexibility: being willing to reconsider a field you'd dismissed as not right for you. This is something Simon Kantor learned when he started looking for a new job after a year out due to the pandemic.

Great new job, no new experience required

Simon Kantor has changed jobs and industries regularly throughout his career. As he puts it, 'I've done a range of things. I'm a bouncy man.'[10]

When the pandemic shuttered schools and day care centres, he and his wife decided that he'd be the one to stay home with their young kids, allowing her to remain focused at her job as a lawyer.

> ***My wife has an amazing career and she's amazing at what she does. My firm was more likely to make a furlough arrangement work. We agreed that it made far more sense for me to take off time.***

(continued)

He took a six-month paid furlough from his communications firm and looked after their children, who were five and one at the time.

During his furlough, he helped his company restructure. As part of that reorganisation, it became clear to his colleagues, and to him, that he'd completed the high-level part of his job, and the role could now be filled with someone less expensive than himself. He left the company, took a six-month severance package, and stayed home for the rest of the pandemic year.

Because he'd moved around a lot, and had the benefit of a good education and varied skills, he wasn't worried about finding a new role. He figured he'd find a new job in a private equity or venture capital firm, and use his operational experience in that way. He called a friend who worked at the global management consulting and executive search firm Egon Zehnder to see if she could help him find a position.

To his surprise, she suggested he apply for a role at Egon Zehnder. No training required.

Executive search? This was not on his radar as a possible career move, or a field he'd thought could ever be right for him.

> ***I always assumed executive search and recruitment was like being a realtor, that they don't really care who does the job as long as a round peg gets put in a round hole.***

He was sceptical, but he agreed to meet some people at the firm and learn more about it. He wound up having 37 interviews – and growing increasingly excited about working in search.

> ***It turns out, I didn't know what I was talking about. It's much more contemplative and strategic. The intimacy of the communication is much different. It's about people, who they want around them to build or grow their business.***

The founder of Egon Zehnder specifically wanted people with varied backgrounds. 'He had the intention of creating a firm that brought insights of a business career into search and consulting. They don't hire people who've done these jobs before.'

Simon got the job, accepted it, and so far, is thrilled with his decision.

> *When I was a consultant, we had to prove why we were in the room, using data. But in this role, it's the quality of conversations that define how good or bad you are. You get to have really, really intimate conversations with people where you uncover their desires and fears. You get to make a real difference and be a trusted adviser during difficult times. I talk to interesting people all day. I'm now paid to do all the stuff I used to do instead of working. It's beautiful.*

Changing jobs can also take stamina. If you're trying to change fields within your own firm, for example, there may be only a few positions that match your skills within your company, and others who are a better match. A young woman I know who wanted to move from sales into product management (like Lisa) applied for one role after another within her firm, and kept being rejected. She built up her product marketing skills by posting well-crafted, thoughtful, product-related content on social media. This got her noticed within the company, but even with that, and with her boss's support and guidance, she couldn't get a hiring manager in product to consider her. She'd been trying for 18 months, which seemed like a long time (especially if you're in your twenties). She felt discouraged and ready to give up.

But then, an opening came up within her company in product marketing that was not as big of a leap in terms of expertise and tenure as the other positions she'd tried for. She applied, and this time, she got the job.

If you want to switch roles, there may be more opportunities outside your company but also stiffer competition. So you will need to persist in either case. Your excitement and curiosity about where you want to go can generate the stamina you need to persist until you get there.

Power Perspective #3: Make one change at a time

If you want to make a career transition, you'll likely have a better shot at getting hired if you switch one aspect of your job at time, rather than aiming for a wholesale career reboot. For example, if you'd like to move to a new role or function (one change), you'll probably have more success if you try to make that switch within your own firm, rather than also seeking a new employer (two changes). You're essentially asking a company to take a risk on you, and this can be easier among people who know you and already value your work.

If you're looking to change companies, industries or sectors (again, one change), applying for jobs similar to the one you currently hold allows you to bring your current skills with you. This is what I did when I went from banking to tech. I was still doing sales, a function in which I had a long, proven track record, but for a new sector. It's much less of a risk for a company to hire someone who has experience, even if it's in a different industry.

It's much less of a risk for a company to hire someone who has experience, even if it's in a different industry.

This is not to say that you couldn't handle changing your role or function *and* your firm, your industry or sector *and* your country of residence all at the same time, but you may have a tough time convincing a hiring manager to take a chance on you.

I was chatting with a guy in Singapore named Ningfei who really wanted to transition from communications to product management. He also wanted to leave his government employer for the private sector and relocate to the US. Ningfei is an impressive and ambitious guy, and he had completed a tech bootcamp, but this three-changes-at-once approach did not generate any job offers. COVID didn't help either.

After repeated rejections, he realised he needed to rank his priorities. He decided that his first goal would be to move into content strategy for digital products. Product management and living in the US could wait. With this plan in mind, he applied for jobs in content strategy in Singapore. He finally landed one in a private firm. (He basically made one-and-a-half changes.)

He's happy with his move and envisions making another change after developing a track record in this new field. I see Ningfei's current plan as an example of someone keeping his eye on his prize – and being realistic about how many moves firms will likely be open to.

Making a change might require additional training. This could be some form of self-directed education, like the young woman who improved and demonstrated her marketing skills by posting product descriptions on social media. But it could also be more formal. During the pandemic, schools, universities and independent training programs all went online. This makes getting retrained easier than ever. You can earn a degree or learn an entirely new field without ever leaving your home. What you don't want to do? Get overwhelmed by the gap between what you know and what you need to know.

In some cases, training is free. After a year of remote counselling during the pandemic, Bianca Blakesely, a clinical social worker in Boston with a master's degree in social work and significant student loan debt, decided not to go back to in-person therapy. She took a coding class online with Code Squad, a free, intensive coding 'camp' geared toward women and people of colour.

She liked it so much that she began coding in her spare time. For her program, she created a directory of hair salons catering to people with Black and natural hair. That led to her starting her own freelance web design company. As she told Boston's local public radio station, WGBH, 'It did take a lot to let go of a previous career, and realize it's OK to make a career change at any stage in your life.'[11]

You may need retraining even at the very beginning of a career, something an aspiring engineer, Erfi Anugrah, learned when seeking his very first job.

New role, same company

I met Erfi, a soft-spoken Singaporean, at Cloudflare in 2018. We hired him as an intern in the marketing department while he was part-way through his degree in business marketing. He was great in his marketing role, and as his internship drew toward its end, we offered him a full-time job in marketing.

But Erfi, it turned out, did not want to work in marketing. After nearly a year at Cloudflare, he had identified his ideal area: solutions engineering. He'd spent a lot of time thinking about the underlying structure of Cloudflare products during his internship. At home, he had experimented with coding, and spent years taking apart machines to see how they worked (often to his mother's distress, he says). Solutions engineering would let him combine his education and interests. 'I felt that this move was something that had been long in the making. Since Cloudflare is a tech company, it seemed like the perfect place to start',[12] he says.

It may have seemed perfect to him, but his background did not make him a natural fit for Cloudflare. Yes, he'd done well in marketing, but engineering is an entirely different field, requiring different, specific skills.

Still, Erfi was excited about this new endeavour. His enthusiasm and curiosity propelled him to find out what skills he'd need for a hiring manager to consider him in solutions engineering.

He talked to the regional head of solutions engineering. This conversation gave him good information about the actual work of an entry-level engineer and clear guidance about the skills he'd have to demonstrate to be considered for a role. He also got some solutions engineer 'homework' – basically figuring out how to solve a specific problem and how to explain why something works or doesn't.

Erfi spent about six months on this homework, developing the proficiency required, then took a Cloudflare test to demonstrate his competence. He passed the test, and was offered an entry-level position in solutions engineering.

He took the job, and is thriving. 'I love that this kind of work is not just about solving problems, which I like to do, but also about being able to explain it in a way that most people can understand', he says.

People much further along in their careers retrain, too. Peter Tonagh, a senior leader with a long career, began as an analyst at BCG and rose to be a CEO. Today, he is a chair and non-executive director at several firms. He doesn't need to learn new skills to succeed; he's already a star. Still, he recently did a training program in data analytics at Harvard, an impressive example of using lifelong learning to stay energised in a long career.

Power Perspective #5: Create momentum where you are

Despite the popularity of job hopping, some firms still have a strong promote-from-within culture, and are large enough to offer continual opportunities to move and rise. You may be able to have a truly dynamic career while staying within one firm, something Korin Kohen has done at Procter & Gamble.

Moving up and overseas within one firm

Korin grew up in Turkey, then studied biochemical engineering at a small, liberal arts college in Pennsylvania, her first time ever in the US. During the summer between her junior and senior year, she got an internship doing research and development in Brussels with the US-based consumer products firm Procter & Gamble. Today, in her mid-thirties, she's still with P&G.

'I literally didn't apply anywhere else', she says.[13] After graduation, she took a job offer at the Brussels office. The firm's approach to

(*continued*)

research and development (R&D) immediately felt like a great fit. 'P&G is a company where R&D also does consumer, market and trend research. Then we do the technical translation of that into a product. I just love that process of innovation – talking to consumers about what their tensions are and being able to offer a solution.'

Korin also likes the company culture and its emphasis on internal communication.

> *P&G is one company where it's normal to stay for 30 years. It's a promote-from-within culture, especially in R&D; they build on expertise. This has created a unique company culture. Everyone has that same understanding that this is a community.*

She's also been able to rise and thrive at P&G because she feels supported by her managers – even in big things like moving across the world.

After five years in Belgium, she wanted to see more of the world, specifically Asia. She'd gotten married by then, and her husband was willing to make the move. Her direct manager helped her investigate options, even though it would mean losing her from his team. 'He contacted his peer in Singapore and the site leadership team. He passed on my résumé. He helped me assess the roles that were available and gave me guidance.'

When she finally found a good position in R&D in Singapore, her manager helped her talk through how to be successful in it.

> *I was doing fabric care in Brussels, working on Downy. Singapore does beauty products, so I would be changing regions and categories, and losing my network. Even though it's the same company, people wouldn't know me. It could have been within my interest to stay in one place, but I wanted the experience. I worked with my manager to say, 'I understand it might not go well, but I want to try'.*

Today, she's still at P&G Singapore, working as a senior director for R&D. She loves managing a team (and her friends love the fact that she sometimes has extra SK-II skincare supplies to share). She says the past 13 years at the same place have given her plenty of opportunities for empowering movement. 'I feel really valued. I have options. I can change assignments. I can move. I never feel I am doing the same thing.'

Occasionally, a person finds themself at the top of their field within their own firm, and yet unable to find a suitable role outside. In this case, you may be able to create a sense of momentum and agency by actively redesigning your current position to include new challenges. This approach is called 'job crafting', and it's a way of becoming a designer of your job, rather than a passive recipient of your title, role and responsibilities. If you'd like to move but can't, job crafting can be an important skill to develop, as Tim Liu has seen in his role.

If you'd like to move but can't, job crafting can be an important skill to develop.

Creating movement in your current job

Tim has been with the same company for seven years. He was the first person hired for their China business, has helped grow the revenue many hundreds of times, and built up a team of almost 50 people. He's proud of his work, but ready for the next big thing.

> ***I've hit my quota 26 out of 28 quarters. It's not just me; it's the whole team. That's pretty amazing, but what's next? When you're doing the same thing for a long time, it's not a challenge anymore. I have 20 more years to work.***

He does a fair amount of job dating and keeps his eye open for opportunities, but he's not very flexible about what he'll accept. He wants to stay in Singapore, with similar responsibilities and without

(*continued*)

decreasing his salary. This means he's at the top of his game in a small field of play.

For now, Tim has decided to change his role without moving on.

> *If I'm hitting my numbers, I can do other things. If I have other ideas that would be good for business, I can propose them. So this is what I'm trying to do.*

His job-crafting efforts include trying to expand his influence beyond mainland China into Taiwan and Hong Kong, and helping the company explore options for other offices throughout APAC. This work lets him get involved in conversations about public policy and government relations, and share his insights and opinions. He's also trying to assert his ideas on issues that impact sales.

> *You need good marketing air cover and partnership opportunities – these things make sales easier. How can I try to influence the leadership in the US and have a bigger say in the function beyond sales?*

Job crafting is helping Tim maintain enthusiasm and energy (which, as you know from chapter 2, are the keys to stamina). Expanding his range in this way is also personally beneficial, and something he recommends to people hoping to move into leadership.

> *At my company, we like people who are 'T-shaped'. This means you have one real strength, one strong pillar, like sales, for me. That's the base of your T. But to take a leadership role, you have to know other things: engineering, HR, finance. Those are the arms of the T. It's worth it to expand into other areas to set yourself up for a leadership role in the future.*

Tim's efforts to stay challenged in his job are commendable. Making a clear decision to stay put is very different from settling into a state of low-grade disappointment and stagnation, what author and University of Pennsylvania, Wharton School psychology professor Adam Grant calls *languishing*. Grant describes languishing as a slow 'dulling of delight' and 'dwindling of drive', an overall feeling of 'blah'. As Grant writes:

> ***Languishing is the neglected middle child of mental health. It's the void between depression and flourishing – the absence of wellbeing ... Languishing dulls your motivation, disrupts your ability to focus and triples the odds that you'll cut back on work.***[14]

Languishing may have been one of the most common states in 2020 and 2021 as people dealt with ongoing fear, anxiety and pandemic-induced limitations and restrictions. But rising and thriving means not letting this feeling overtake your career, even if you are 'stuck' in your current job for the time being.

Job crafting can help. As a 2020 survey on job crafting conducted by four professors in England and Australia found, actively redesigning your job can notably improve your engagement. To test how much job crafting improves engagement, and to provide guidance for managers supporting employees' efforts, the researchers interviewed 1000 business leaders and 2000 of their employees in Australia, the UK and North America. Their findings are impressive. They revealed that, of the study participants who job-crafted, two-thirds 'felt inspired to stretch past their comfort zones and engage in active cooperation with other colleagues, leading to a more connected workforce'; 92 per cent were more satisfied at work and at home, leading to a notable decrease in stress; and staff turnover decreased by 29 per cent within firms that used job crafting, because 'Active crafters were more likely to stay put and adjust their role rather than move elsewhere'.

As a leader, you can help your employees find ways to put more of themselves into their work, and you should. 'I'm asking my team to come up with new projects', Tim says about his own efforts to help others do this. 'People are very smart here; they get their job description done and then they're bored. So how do we keep them motivated? How can we get them to do different projects, things that are completely different?'

Takeaways

- Interests change; your career path can change with them. You are not locked into the industry, sector, job or location in which you began. Be open to new desires and pursue them.
- Prepare for your promotion, then ask. Demonstrating that you can do the job you desire helps your manager move you up.
- Be flexible and persistent when seeking a career change.
- Try to make one change at a time – instead of two or three – to facilitate movement.
- You can create momentum within your own firm or even within your job. Staying put does not have to mean languishing or being stuck.

mindshift six

Distant is the new diverse: Include the international and working-from-home team

Power perspectives in this chapter

- let your thirst for adventure turbocharge your career
- remove the R from remote (as in, emote)
- choreograph opportunities for relationships to develop.

I met Sierra Dasso in 2018 at the Cloudflare headquarters in San Francisco during a work trip. I'd taken the 15-hour flight from Singapore to California, as I'd been doing about four times a year since moving back to Singapore. It's one of my favourite flights because it meets my need for efficiency. Not only can I get a lot of work done and still catch a movie, but because it crosses the International Date Line, at certain times of the year, I can also land just before I left.

While in California on that trip, I spoke at a company lunch for women in sales. I was the company's most senior woman in sales, and it was still somewhat uncommon to have women in senior sales roles, particularly in 'enterprise', or large company, business-to-business. I was glad for the chance to encourage other women to envision themselves in sales leadership roles in the future.

The Cloudflare office had a typical start-up vibe: four floors of exposed brick and open space. Conference rooms were named for HTTP error codes. The lunch was held in the largest conference room, logically named after the most common error code, 404. However, Room 404 was confusingly located on the *first* floor, making it very hard for newcomers to find. (You have to be savvy to make it in tech. Or at least make it to the meetings.)

About 20 women came to the meeting, everyone seating themselves around a big, rectangular table. Others dialled in from various parts of the world. After the meeting, I returned to the desk I was using and checked my emails. I saw a message from Sierra, saying she'd been at the meeting and was so inspired by my description of living in Asia and the idea of working for a woman that she wanted to come work in our Singapore office. I always wax eloquent about living in different countries when I give talks; I was delighted that someone else seemed to have caught my enthusiasm for living overseas.

I got up and walked over to her desk, finding an American in her late twenties, with a friendly, girl-next-door attitude. 'I want to live in Asia, too!' she said.

We needed salespeople in Asia, as it happened, to cover countries including Thailand, Japan and Indonesia. But they needed to speak one of the relevant languages, which she didn't. I said, 'What about Australia?' I also oversaw Australia as part of APAC for Cloudflare. I thought it would be good to have an account executive there who could bring the company culture and know-how with her.

I knew she'd have a good shot at success in an English-speaking country with a similar culture to her own. (I know that Australia has its own distinct culture that is very different from the US; as an American married to an Aussie, this fact has been drummed into me. On the other hand, our cultures have fused in many ways. Stories circulate of Australians going to court and 'pleading the Fifth!' as in, the Fifth Amendment to the US Constitution, which has no bearing on Australian law but does appear regularly on US courtroom dramas on TV.)

Sierra was not excited about Australia. It seemed like just another Western country. 'Not exotic.' She was also concerned that she wouldn't succeed because she didn't think Australia was known for having tech companies, the types of firms she was selling to in the US.

I completely disagreed with her assessment that there wasn't enough opportunity in tech. What about Atlassian, Canva and Afterpay? I also thought she'd love the country, as I do.

She decided to try. Sierra transferred to the Sydney office in 2019. Within a year, she had a car, a dog, a wonderful partner – and a great deal of success at work. While the similarities between the US and Australia helped her make new connections easily, the fact that the industry is smaller in Australia proved to be a bonus.

> ***Now that I've been here a while, I know all the companies. As soon as I say I know someone they know or I worked with their competitor, I'm 10 steps ahead in that relationship in terms of it being fruitful. Also, the US is much more independent. Here, it is more collective. That's a good thing for me in sales because if we sell to one company, then another company in that industry wants to use us, too.[1]***

Sierra quickly became a huge fan of the Australian lifestyle, too. 'The overall standard of living is significantly higher than in California. I also love the beauty of the country, the international vibe and the expat community', she says. 'And the government really values life, which is nice.'

The 'Ah-ha!' of Sierra's story: be open to where in the world your career may take you

Australia wasn't Singapore, Sierra's initial dream, but it *was* a huge international move that expanded her world view and enhanced her life – her real aims. Moving to the Sydney office offered professional opportunities she had not expected, and likely would not have gotten as quickly had she stayed in headquarters.

Today, many firms operate on a global scale, and this opens up opportunities for success and adventure in countries around the world, even in places you may never have considered exploring. Being willing to relocate can be a springboard to more responsibility and lead to quicker advancement. This is one more way in which your work and your life are on the same team. You don't necessarily have to choose between living in Paris, say, and building valuable skills at work. You may be able to do both at the same time.

It's true that during the pandemic, and after, many countries limited the number of work visas and focused on developing ways to connect through virtual meetings. Some also pursued more local talent. But opportunities to work overseas still exist, and likely will into the future. Not everyone can do a stint overseas, of course. Fields requiring state or federal licensing, like medicine or law, are not easily transportable, and plenty of people have family or other obligations that keep them put. But if you can swing it, opportunities for adventure abound.

Not only can an international position be exciting, but it also helps you understand the cultures, experiences and perspectives of people in different countries. An international assignment lets you see, first-hand, that another office isn't 'remote'; it's right at the centre of a different map. Success increasingly requires being able to cooperate with those halfway around the world.

I'm personally invested in diversity and inclusion and have been throughout my career, and I see these terms as also applying to people in diverse locations. Embracing diversity and inclusion in this context means thinking beyond your national borders, being inclusive of those from different nations, and considering how working in another country might enhance your career. It also means remembering that people in offices thousands of miles away are essential members of the company; developing an inclusive mindset; and practising the skills needed to remain connected across time zones, oceans and cultural differences. Here's how.

Power Perspective #1: Let your thirst for adventure turbocharge your career

The search for talent has gone global, and capitalising on this trend can be a great way to accelerate your rise. While moving overseas for work may sound like a dream to you, your willingness to go is also very helpful for your firm. An organisation benefits from having someone on board who wants to be transferred overseas, and not everyone is willing to do it. You become a 'culture carrier' for the company, an ambassador steeped in the firm's culture who can help build global cohesiveness.

In an office filled only with new hires, unfamiliar with the organisation's culture and protocols, tasks take longer, even small things, like figuring out how to enter information in the company's database. Your knowledge of how things are done at headquarters can boost the effectiveness of regional offices, helping them meet corporate goals.

You become a 'culture carrier' for the company, an ambassador steeped in the firm's culture who can help build global cohesiveness.

Having diverse perspectives around the table also boosts the bottom line, in part because making room for different outlooks leads to more creative problem-solving. A recent study from BCG looking at diversity among employees at 1700 companies in eight countries across a variety of industries and sizes suggests that 'increasing the diversity of leadership teams leads to more and better innovation and improved financial performance'. In the study, innovation benefited most from leadership teams that included diversity in national origin of executives, a range of industry backgrounds, gender balance and a variety of career paths.[2]

In other words, diversity includes national origin and is good for business. In turn, international experience is good for you and for your company.

Understanding and valuing different perspectives is not only the right thing to do, but is also an increasingly important competency at work. Malini Vaidya, Head of APAC for Spencer Stuart, a global executive search and leadership consulting firm, says:

> ***There is no question that global thinking and sensitivity is fuelled by experiences living and working in more than one country – not just through managing a regional or global role from one country your entire career. The more senior you become, the more likely you will need a track record of managing across borders and cultures.***[3]

Rahul Desai, the sales operations guru I met at the Google headquarters in Mountain View and offered a job while going through a revolving door in Beijing (chapter 3), is a perfect example of the career boost that can come from overseas work. Because he came to new, small office, he had the chance to take on tasks that would have been the specific job description of other people back in San Francisco. These experiences built real skills and breadth that enabled him to rise faster.

While his job was intended to only be an 18-month assignment, he wound up staying in Singapore for nine years, first at Google and then at Facebook, rising into management. He eventually moved back to Texas, taking all his management experience with him. Later, he was offered a great job as vice president of sales strategy and operations at Trip Actions (a travel management and expense company), a position he likely would not have gotten without that overseas experience, and the demands and opportunities it created.

Working in a culture different from your own definitely brings new challenges, as Stacy Brown-Philpot, a former colleague and adventurous, highly successful corporate leader, discovered when she moved to India. As Stacy saw, figuring out exactly what you need to make an international move work for you can propel your advancement – and help you develop the habit of identifying your needs and asking for them.

Taking a chance on change and making it work

Stacy Brown-Philpot was managing a large operations team at Google in San Francisco when an opportunity arose that seemed too good to pass up – the chance to become senior director of online sales and operations for Google, India.

Stacy always had wanted to work overseas, and running the office would be an amazing opportunity. But she had a couple of real concerns. India was a very different culture, and she suspected that leading there could be tough.

> ***I'd travelled to India many times, but the thought of living and working there was much more daunting. Not only was there a new language and culture to consider, but India's classically male-dominated environment wouldn't be easy for an African-American woman to navigate.***[4]

She had another concern: her husband wasn't in a position to relocate with her, so taking the job would mean living apart for a year. She and her husband wanted to start a family, and the move would put this on hold, too.

Stacy and her husband talked about the opportunity and the prospect of living apart. They knew separation can be very tough on marriage and that it would delay them starting a family. They spent time figuring out what they would need from the company

(*continued*)

to make it work. Stacy presented these terms to her manager and got the company's buy-in. Then, Stacy moved to India alone.

As she later told *The New York Times*:

> ***India was a really important market for Google at the time, and I knew they were going to take care of me. So we decided together, as a couple, to delay the decision to start a family so I could take this career opportunity.***[5]

Running the India office definitely posed a big learning curve, which she welcomed. In India, she had to adapt her management style to fit the culture, being less consensus driven and more directive. It was an adjustment, but as she tells it, having grown up defending herself from bullies in Detroit taught her the skill of speaking up.

When she returned to the US, she went on to run the operations team for Google, overseeing 600 people from a big corner office. After about nine years, she realized it was time to move on and do something new in her career. She made the switch to TaskRabbit (an organisation matching freelance talent with local jobs), where she became CEO. Today Stacy is a founding member of SoftBank's Opportunity Fund, a $100 million fund that invests in Black, Latinx and Native American founders. She also serves on the boards of StockX, Noom, Nordstrom and HP.

More than a decade later, she looked back on her India experience and the plan she made with her husband as a pivotal learning moment in her career. 'I ended up having an amazing experience.' She and her husband are still married and have two daughters.

Today's increasingly hybrid and/or remote workforce means some people are taking their laptops to their dream locales and setting up shop there. If you have this opportunity, I do think it will allow you to gain a more global perspective to some degree. But working alone with a view of the ocean from Playa del Carmen, Mexico, is a different experience to working in or leading a multicultural team in a country not your own. I see the notion of 'have laptop; will travel', as more akin to working from home, but from a home base that you find more exciting or less expensive or closer to family. This won't necessarily give you the career boost of relocating to a different office with your firm, but it will expand your cultural competence and cultural humility.

Here's how to get your firm to support your thirst for adventure.

Have passport; will transfer

You can be the solution to your firm's need for overseas talent. Here's how to organise a transfer within your firm.

- **Educate yourself.** Look for open positions on your firm's intranet, and talk to people currently working in those locations about their experience. Ask what they like about the office and their role. What's challenging? Do they think your skills are transferable? Will you need to speak the language to succeed?
- **Enlist your boss.** While it's fine to do 'job dating' outside of your firm without telling your boss, if you want to move within your firm, you do need to share this desire. Your boss should support you, and may have the connections and information to help make it possible. Your boss is also the person who can give you a good reference. A furtive inquiry will likely get back to your boss anyway; better to be up front than risk your relationship.
- **Help your employees move.** If you are in a leadership position, it is your job to help your employees grow in their careers, even if this means helping them move to a different country. This benefits the employee and the company – and is part of building and maintaining social capital.

If you have a family, be open to how your move may benefit them. When Rahul transferred to Singapore, his wife, an artist, learned batik, a new technique for her, and incorporated it into her work. In my case, my husband, Linton, has been willing to move for my career. He's found jobs in each location, and focused on enjoying the adventure, appreciating our kids' ability to gain a global perspective, and supporting my goals. Our sons have grown up with a sense of themselves as 'globosapiens', which is really important to us.

If your partner or spouse has an opportunity to transfer overseas, be open to how this might benefit *you*. You might be surprised by what the move will do for your own career, as Crystal Hayling, a non-profit professional with an impressive track record, discovered when she moved to Asia with her husband.

Supporting a partner's move and benefitting along the way

In 2009, Crystal Hayling was serving as the CEO of the Blue Shield Foundation of California, the philanthropic arm of Blue Shield of California. It was a dream job that she'd landed after a long, successful career in the non-profit arena. She'd been at the Blue Shield Foundation for five years, during which time she'd grown it into one of the largest funders of domestic violence prevention programs in California, giving out nearly $40 million a year in grants. 'I loved that job', she says. 'I loved doing grant-making work and public policy around universal healthcare and domestic violence.'[6]

But then her husband had a chance to move to Singapore for two years with his job at Apple, a great career opportunity for him. Living overseas was also a dream for Crystal and her husband. 'Both of us had lived outside of the country as adults, prior to meeting each other, and it had been really formative for us. We really wanted that for our kids.'

Crystal made the decision to leave her job in order to go to Asia and support her husband's career. She felt she could probably benefit from a break, but it was scary to step out of her career.

> *I'd started my job at Blue Shield with a three-month old and a toddler, a very intense time to have been doing the start-up*

thing. It had been a fantastic run, but I also realised: it will not be the worst thing in the world for me to shift, and take some time for my kids. Someone has to be a primary parent, and my husband and I have ebbed and flowed about who is primary parent. I had to have confidence in myself to know that I could do it and still get back into my career.

When she arrived in Singapore, Crystal quickly saw how dynamic the nascent philanthropic sector in Asia was. Families with newly minted fortunes needed help organising their giving strategies. Crystal had valuable expertise. She'd intended to spend time with her kids and write and think. She did this, but she also joined the board of a new family foundation. Then she started advising other family foundations and family philanthropic efforts. She led a research project, published a big report and joined a second board.

She wasn't working in a full-time, organisational role, but she was working hard and learning a tremendous amount about the world of family philanthropy.

Her whole family loved living in Asia. 'We had a phenomenal experience', she says. Two years extended into six.

The thing they don't tell you about being an expat is that the hardest part isn't deciding to go, but to come back. If you're having a wonderful experience, it feels great to keep going. But I want my kids to be Americans. I'm African-American. It's important to me that my kids understand what that means and who we are and what we fight for. Particularly because I do social justice work.

As their oldest son was about to enter seventh grade, they decided it was time to go back to California. For Crystal, this meant returning to her career. 'It was terrifying to come back. It felt like I had been out of the field for a long time.'

She spent the first six months in the US reconnecting through social media platforms and in person, and rebuilding her network.

(*continued*)

She was offered a job at the Aspen Institute starting a new environmental fellowship program, a step down from her previous full-time position, but a good way to return to the industry in the US.

Then she got a call about a leadership position at the Libra Foundation, a private philanthropic foundation started by the Pritzker family. Could she lead a family foundation? She'd never done that before, but she had just spent six years working closely with families starting foundations. 'When the headhunter called me about this job, I was like, "I guess I do have experience working with families".'

For Crystal, supporting her husband's move expanded her skills in tremendously valuable ways, particularly given the fact that family foundations have become increasingly powerful in the US, too. Crystal met the family, loved them and got the job – a new dream job. 'Here I am, running a pretty significant family foundation. The work I did in Asia with families helped prepare me, unexpectedly, for this.'

Power Perspective #2: Remove the 'R' from remote (as in, *emote*)

Having spent the past 25 years running parts, or all, of the APAC business for Google, Twitter, Cloudflare and other companies, I've seen first-hand how professionally and personally rewarding it can be to work outside your home country. But I've also observed how challenging it can be to stay emotionally connected to the company and its leadership when you're outside headquarters – and the critical role that this emotional connection plays. This is true whether you're at the start of your career, further along or leading multiple teams dispersed across the globe, as I have.

We all need to feel emotionally connected to our company, our jobs and our colleagues. People collaborate better across functions when they feel close to others, despite physical distance. People are more productive when they feel valued and recognised. People stay longer with firms that make them feel cared about and important. Whether you're at headquarters, in an office halfway around the globe, or working from home, staying connected means removing the 'r' from 'remote', as in *emote*.

Focusing on emotional connection is also a key to thriving.

I think of this as a leadership skill; to remain competitive, leaders at firms across the planet need to dial up their focus on the emotional connection between people in headquarters and employees working outside the main office. But as an individual contributor working overseas, focusing on emotional connection is also a key to thriving. Here's how.

Make room for the human factor

During the pandemic-related shutdown, when a delivery person might have arrived in the middle of a meeting, inciting a barking fit from an employee's dog, or when a child's teacher scheduled an at-home cooking project requiring adult supervision during the workday, it was impossible not to notice that teams are composed of real people, with real, human needs. This is one benefit of the pandemic's enforced work-from-home period: all leaders had a chance to see (or were unable to escape) the humanity of their teams.

I think of this as acknowledging the human factor, and it's an important part of removing the 'r' from remote.

One of the easiest and most important ways to acknowledge the human factor of those on international teams is to check their time zone. I am constantly dumbfounded by the number of people who fail to consider the time zone difference between their location and that of the people they are meeting.

I once had a person at headquarters in California schedule a call for 6 am Singapore time – not an hour I would ever choose to be at work, though I was willing to get up to accommodate the time zone difference. I woke up early, made a cup of tea, and dragged myself to the computer, only to find out that he'd cancelled the meeting at the last minute to go to a kid's soccer game. I'm glad he was able to do that, but I could have gotten a couple more hours of (much needed) beauty sleep. When I mentioned the inconvenience later (as nicely as possible), the person said, 'I let you know I was cancelling three hours ago'. *Three hours ago was 3 am my time, and I was not on email!* This kind of obliviousness to what time it is somewhere else is an ongoing gripe of people working overseas – and one very easy to address by a five-second Internet search.

As a dispersed worker, it's up to you to set boundaries around your time. Share them in a way that emphasises your desire to excel. You could say, 'These midnight meetings are threatening my productivity the next day, and I really want to make sure I'm delivering my best'.

Then offer a solution. You might say, 'Let's prioritise. Pick the most important meeting for me to be at each week, and I'll attend that one, and shift my start time to later the next day'. Or, 'I don't mind starting meetings at 6 am and exposing my bedhead once a week, but I can't do it every day. Let me delegate the other meetings to someone else on my team, who can also learn from them.' You can even propose that those in headquarters occasionally stretch to do a meeting that suits your time zone.

There are plenty of other ways that a lack of boundaries around time can compromise the productivity of distributed or home-based workers – such as having an unspoken expectation that people be available online day and night. As a leader, you can help your team set boundaries around time by implementing new communication norms.

When the pandemic sent his workforce of 130 people home, Drew Sanocki, then-CEO of the San Diego–based online automotive aftermarket products company AutoAnything, realised that his employees were suddenly on email and Slack day and night, seven days a week. Work was taking over their lives, compromising their effectiveness and happiness.

> ***There's a lot of research showing that ready access to instant communication makes us less productive and less happy, and prevents knowledge workers from engaging in highly productive work. We saw this happening. I started tracking my own time and realised all day long I'd be on Instant Messenger chatting with my employees, interrupting their days.[7]***

To solve this new problem generated by working remotely, AutoAnything established new norms of behaviour to control technology use. The firm also set expectations around communication, including discouraging the use of Slack or email before noon or after six, other than for social reasons. 'We wanted to reserve the hours from nine to noon for deep thinking, solving problems, creating new marketing campaigns – the heavy brain activity', Sanocki says.

His company also experimented with 'batching' communication, rather than letting endless text threads run throughout the day; encouraging phone calls rather than text messages for quick questions; scheduling team meetings to answer questions all at one time; and having those in high demand set office hours, rather than being open on chat all the time.

These guidelines proved immediately beneficial. Sanocki says:

> ***In the one group we measured, IT, the number of tickets they went through rose each week, big time. Anecdotally, I feel like the company is making more progress on its strategic initiatives. Chat is more for socialising and less for work, which is nice.***

Sanocki says his company plans to remain all-virtual, and to keep these boundaries in place to help employees stay productive and not feel stressed out by what could otherwise be a never-ending work day. Establishing new norms has to start with the leadership team, meaning Sanoki has to follow his own guidelines. 'So far, it's working really well.'

Acknowledging the human factor *before a person asks* can generate strong loyalty. A Singapore-based communications professional at a large US tech firm said to me recently, 'My new manager offered to move an 11 pm call earlier for me, even though I'm the only person on her time in APAC. I love this new manager and I'm never leaving her.'

Sometimes a firm or boss will really go out of their way to acknowledge the human factor, such as helping support an employee through a particularly challenging time. As Kate Fleming saw in Singapore, this emotional connection can be so valuable that it might inspire a person to stay with the firm even if offered a higher salary elsewhere.

Generating more loyalty than money can buy

Kate Fleming is an Australian with an honest, disarming attitude. During the pandemic, she set up a beautiful background in her house for virtual meetings, with matching white planters, healthy green plants, and artfully arranged books. When complimented on her space during a call, she laughed and moved the camera to show the rest of the room where she'd piled up everything else that didn't 'work' within the frame. She's poised, and confident enough to let down her guard.

She was working at an Internet company in Singapore in early 2021 as the director of customer success, APAC, overseeing 21 people. She had one child, a young daughter named Grace. Then, when trying to get pregnant again, she found herself dealing with infertility. 'I came to the parenting nirvana very late', she says. 'I was 37 when I had my daughter. I hadn't spent much time thinking about my life beyond career.'[8]

But now she was thinking about it, and trying to build her family. She underwent fertility treatment, and the first round of IVF didn't work, which took a toll on her mentally and physically, and brought added friction into her household, which her working hours made impossible to address. After what she calls, 'another IVF disaster', she realised that her 24/7 workday was untenable at that point in her life.

She shared her frustration with her boss. 'I was like, "Guys, I'm really struggling. I'm running out of options here. I need to time to figure out what we're going to do".' She decided to resign and accepted a role with the promise of a greater work-life balance from an inspiring leader at Google, where she was also offered better pay.

But her direct manager, the company's chief commercial officer, did not want to lose her, and quickly mobilised support from key executives in the business, and even one of the company's founders, to find a way to keep her in the company.

> ***They said, 'Why don't you do something that has more predictable hours so you can have family time and focus on the family front for now? We're going to find you a role with a little more breathing space.'***

They came back to her with a proposal, helping to coordinate the company's 'Back to Better' initiative, designed to help bring people back to the office post-pandemic, and foster the rebuilding of community and connections between different teams and departments.

It was less money than the competing offer, and a step back from leading a team to being an individual contributor. But the chance to stay with a firm that would make such an effort for her made it worth it.

> ***The other role offered some very appealing benefits and presented the chance to work for one of the coolest names in tech, but it didn't include this kind of personal understanding. These were people who were, and still are, senior leaders in a hypergrowth company who have better things to do than worry about helping me have a second child. But they took the time and energy to try to find a way to keep me in the company that aligned with what I needed. You can't buy that kind of support.***

You probably cannot simply ask for a major accommodation in your role, and expect the company to grant it – unless you've shown that you are a real asset. As Kate says:

> ***They said they felt I'd shown commitment in the two-and-a-half years I'd been with the company. I absolutely had not been slouching. You have to put in the work first, build that trust or consistency of delivering, so that when you do need help, people know you're genuine. It can't be three months and then you go in and say, 'Listen, I want you to give me a special allowance'. You also have to be incredibly lucky to have the right kind of manager, and company leadership, to be willing to lean in to a long-term employee-employer relationship like that.***

It was also a time when companies around the globe were losing employees, making concessions, and seeing how working from home and other new approaches could work. Timing can play a part in getting what you ask for.

My co-writer, Wendy, asked to work Fridays at home at her *Psychology Today* editing job only three months after taking it, when there was a glut of unemployed journalists. She had a new baby and, like Kate, had gone to a lot of effort to get pregnant. She also had a long commute, and there was not a lot of interaction among editors within the office anyway. Four days in the office made sense to her.

The owner of the company did not agree. He refused to allow any flexibility in the schedule, for anyone. 'I realise now that I hadn't built a track record at all. I hadn't proven my worth', Wendy says. 'There were hundreds or maybe thousands of journalists out of work in the area, so he had no incentive to make any special concessions to me.'

She wound up leaving the job.

> ***I went back in before I left and said to him that psychology was actually a specialised body of knowledge and I had a lot of experience writing about it and I thought he was making a mistake. He did not budge, and while I felt disappointed, I was glad I'd at least said what I thought.***

She was out of work for a while, though she wrote a few articles for *Psychology Today* as a freelancer. 'I felt like I'd left the last staff journalism job on the planet. I definitely did some second-guessing about that decision', she says. She volunteered to do communications work for a couple of non-profits supporting artisans in the developing world to gain communications experience, and then landed a fellowship through Encore.org to be the director of communications at a non-profit called Sustainable South Bronx. That job led her to realise that she definitely didn't want to do communications. She wound up selling a book idea to Simon & Schuster and has been writing books ever since.

Remember that all employees are created equal (regardless of where they sit)

Ignoring other people's time zones reflects a larger, common problem that can hinder cooperation in international firms – treating offsite employees like second-class citizens. This shows up not only in terms of time insensitivity but also in compensation packages and basic protections.

One company I worked for offered overseas workers an inferior healthcare package to that given to US-based employees in equivalent roles. This action undermined employees' enthusiasm and loyalty, and affected their performance. Desired recruits chose other multinational firms instead, ones that gave Asia-based employees equal benefits. (It also ate up my time as I spent a year campaigning for the firm to improve healthcare coverage.)

Another way that some firms treat those in regional offices like second-class citizens is by failing to effectively allocate resources. This isn't necessarily intentional; it's easy to overlook the needs of those you don't see in front of you every day. But it feels dismissive, erodes trust and loyalty, and hinders performance. It's hard to perform when you don't have the resources you need. Employees and leaders are likely to ask themselves, 'Why stay at a firm that doesn't help me succeed?'

As a leader of a dispersed team, you often have to fight for resources your team needs to do their job. It's important to maintain your stamina for what can be an ongoing source of frustration. My strategy is to make my priorities clear, back them up with data and persist.

Another way of getting those in headquarters to think about your projects is to include them in the planning. Korin Kohen, in research and development at P&G, has found that bringing in others from the beginning ups their sense of urgency. It's a great way of 'rallying the team. You need to influence people to prioritise your project, to get the experts to support it, and the team to work coherently together', she says.[9]

Including others from the start helps, and leads to better innovation. 'If you engage people from the beginning in the journey, you are more likely to get a better product.'

Research backs up the value of diverse thinking in innovation. That same BCG report (from p.138) showed that companies reporting above-average diversity on their management teams also reported innovation revenue that was 19 percentage points higher than that of companies with below average leadership diversity – 45 per cent of total revenue versus just 26.

Leaders can help global employees feel seen and valued during company-wide meetings by highlighting success stories from around the world. A US-based company, for example, could focus on Union Pay instead of Mastercard, Uniqlo instead of Gap, and Nestlé rather than General Foods, when sharing client examples.

Finally, another way of treating all employees equally is to learn about, and be sensitive to, the unique aspects of their culture. Cultural norms dramatically affect priorities and expectations. Leaders and employees should build their 'cultural competence', knowledge about and understanding of other cultures – and also develop 'cultural humility'. Cultural humility describes having an attitude of genuine openness and curiosity about cultures that are different from your own. Showing cultural humility means continually learning about the values, habits, experiences and desires of those in different countries, and working *with* their culture. It also means acknowledging that other people are the experts of their own lives and have valuable insights to contribute.

When I led the APAC division for various companies, I made an effort to share the region's culture with those visiting from the home office or working in other locations. I aimed for light, fun approaches, such as sending small, funny gifts from the region to thank people for their efforts, like sushi erasers from Japan or batik napkins from Indonesia.

For years, I hosted a Durian Challenge, offering visitors the chance to taste this highly prized (smelly) delicacy, often called the 'king of fruits' in Asia (yet described in far less glowing terms by some due to its strong, dare I say, noxious smell). The durian is so malodorous that it's a prohibited substance in many taxis across Asia. The Durian Challenge was a fun way to introduce people to this unique fruit and help people let down their guard.

One standing activity at one of the companies I worked at is a monthly birthday celebration. In Asia, we created a culturally inclusive variation on this, singing happy birthday in the native language of those celebrating that month. During the pandemic, these birthday parties went virtual. We delivered a slice of cake to the home of each person celebrating and then came together online to sing in everyone's language. Even things that seem rote when everyone is working together in headquarters (like licking frosting off a plastic knife with colleagues) can serve as important bonding moments for dispersed workers.

Over communicate

In a distributed or hybrid work environment, it's very easy for information to fall through the cracks. The solution: over communicate.

Silicon Valley tech firms are generally excellent at keeping people around the globe up to date and informed through weekly virtual 'town halls'. Groups from across the globe share updates, and executive leaders talk about strategy or a recent board meeting. This communication is valuable, but it doesn't replace one-on-one conversation.

While you may be loath to have more meetings, when there's limited personal contact, virtual time together helps ensure that people feel included and informed, rather than isolated. To the extent possible given the size of teams, leaders should aim for some small way to engage one-on-one with new joiners and with existing employees. As a regional leader, I met with everyone who joined APAC for half an hour within their first few months, even if I was never going to work with them directly, to help them feel connected to the firm and its leadership.

Team innovation can also be difficult in a dispersed work environment. For Korin Kohen, communication supports the development of new ideas and products.

If you say, 'Okay, now I'm going to sit down and come up with an idea!' it probably won't come. You get more inspiration and ideas by talking to people and learning what's been done before. You need to be able to spark, to have catalysts. Innovation rarely comes when you sit down alone and work.

Make more time for recognition than seems necessary

When working with or overseeing people away from headquarters, anything you want to have happen must be planned, and this includes acknowledging your team's victories – to them and to others. Praise makes people feel valued and seen, emotions that create connection. Praise is often in short supply for people working far from managers and team members, whether in a regional office or at home.

Leaders should recognise and celebrate dispersed employees' efforts more than seems necessary.

If you oversee people who you rarely or never interact with in person, it takes extra effort to make your appreciation felt. Make this effort. I'm not suggesting telling everyone how awesome they are all the time if they're messing up, but leaders should recognise and celebrate dispersed employees' efforts *more than seems necessary*.

When you see great work, take the time to shoot off a complimentary email to the responsible team, and maybe even their manager. This cheers the group, and models behaviour for others to follow.

You also need to make sure that decision-makers *beyond your office and region* see your employees' great work. Mentioning their names during meetings helps, but it can take more than a virtual high-five to get dispersed workers truly known by those in power. Rahul Desai says:

It's difficult to develop a strong professional reputation at headquarters when nobody knows who you are or what you do. It's easy for headquarters to develop bias in favour of those whose work is more readily visible to them.

This translates into better opportunities and promotions for those working in headquarters.

To combat location-related bias, Rahul not only offers virtual public praise, but he also talks about specific employees by name in conversations with headquarters, and he creates opportunities for them that will generate recognition. This can take a lot of thoughtfulness, but it's a mark of a really strong leader.

In one case, Rahul realised that the weekly revenue forecasting process was taking a full Monday for the team to do. 'I thought it was ridiculous to have someone sitting there for eight hours basically copying and pasting data', he says. He asked an operations guy on his team to see if he could automate the process. This employee created a program that cut the process from eight hours to 30 minutes. Rahul then let everyone in headquarters know what this employee had developed.

> ***I could have just sat on this development and been happy that it worked well for Asia Pacific. Instead, I was very vocal about it and made others in headquarters and my counterparts in Europe aware of what was being done here, that he was the developer behind it, and that it saved time and energy.***

This effort gained the employee recognition across the whole organisation. Rahul went a step further and encouraged him to develop the program for other offices.

> ***I said to everyone else, 'We can produce this for you in Singapore, and because we're ahead of you time-wise, we can have it in your inbox when you arrive Monday morning'.***

His employee developed it to scale for the rest of the world and helped other offices implement it. This became part of his job, along with maintaining the report. 'He became known as the person behind that report', says Rahul. 'We wound up hiring two more developers to report to him and they took on some other global reporting tasks under his leadership.'

Even as an individual contributor, you can help create a culture of recognition. The 'peer bonus' funds that Google lets employees give each other (chapter 3) is a great way to encourage everyone on the team to recognise others (everyone likes receiving praise in the form of cash). But you don't need a formal peer bonus program to share your appreciation for a colleague.

Power Perspective #3: Choreograph opportunities for connection

Korin Kohen says so much of her day is spent in virtual meetings, her husband often asks when she gets her work done.

> ***He looks at my calendar and is like, 'Why are you talking all day? When do you do work?' I have Monday and Wednesday nights blocked for half-hour, one-on-one meetings with my partners in the innovation ecosystem, mostly in Cincinnati. Then I do the same with the team in Singapore, meeting in person, when we can.***[10]

Her actual work? That gets done 'between meetings', Korin says.

Except that all these meetings are a vital part of her job because they create connection. As is true with the regular reviews and group meetings she also has scheduled, these one-on-one get-togethers let her update people in the US and Japan on happenings in her office, represent her team and their efforts, and build and maintain real rapport.

> ***I think P&G has a meeting disease, but it's a survival mechanism in a place so big. You have to make the effort to build relationships. When you are not in the mothership, you need to work twice as hard to be heard, to get support, and to stay top of mind.***

Careers are not just built by competency — they are built by connection. Typically, you can build these connections inside a company organically. You grab lunch or an after-work drink with someone at the next desk, which may lead to a project down the road. You speak up in a team meeting, and a manager comes into your office afterwards to follow up on your idea.

When it comes to the benefit of working together in person, I always think of the term 'collaboration dividend'. It's generally used to describe working together across networks, silos or countries with the aid of technology. But I've also heard it used in relation to the value of working together in person, an acknowledgement of how even casual conversations can give rise to improved output. You get a bonus, or a *dividend*, from time spent together in person.

Careers are not just built by competency – they are built by connection.

Distance means you lose out on this naturally occurring rapport. It also can deplete your social capital, as many people saw during the pandemic. Embracing global diversity means taking steps to choreograph opportunities for connection for your team, if you're a leader, and for yourself.

It can be done. As Joseph Grenny, co-founder of Vitalsmarts, a Utah-based leadership training and online career education platform, puts it:

> ***For decades, studies of corporate culture have concluded that the further two people were apart physically, the lower their estimation of one another was likely to be. Our findings suggest otherwise – distance isn't destiny.*[11]**

Grenny is referring to a recent study he co-authored that looked at steps leaders took, or failed to take, to preserve a shared company culture during the pandemic. His team asked study participants to report on five behaviours linked to healthy group performance, including responding quickly to requests from each other, giving co-workers the benefit of the doubt and sacrificing their own needs to serve a larger team goal.

In companies where leaders made efforts to preserve shared culture, these behaviours and attitudes survived. In companies where leaders didn't, respondents reported being quicker to be suspicious of others' motives, slower to respond to colleagues' needs, more narrowly focused on their own interests and less willing to put in extra time or effort to get things done. In other words, their trust and support of each other deteriorated.

Grenny's team concluded that, while efforts to preserve culture and social capital while remote don't have to be difficult, they are important. Some examples cited in the study include:

- implementing new tools and technology to facilitate connection
- sponsoring and supporting fun, off-the-wall, virtual events
- scheduling non-work-related meetings for team members to get together.

These are easy, sometimes fun, ways to help employees connect and remain seen by each other and by leaders. BCG Australia took a collaborative, employee-led approach to designing ways to support work and foster strong connections, post-COVID. One idea the teams came up with was to ask to work together in person at least half the time, if possible, to promote productivity and deliver on the company's apprenticeship model. Another idea was to have hybrid teams on the same schedule; basically everyone is in the office or at home at the same time.[12]

Getting together in person for fun activities is also part of BCG's plan. Activities that help people connect include a monthly 'Big Friday' event in the office, with catered breakfast and lunch; team yoga; and an extra emphasis on encouraging people to attend offsite group outings and retreats.

Making an effort to stay connected with people you don't see every day also can be key to pushing difficult projects to completion across multiple time zones. Batsheva Lazarus, a former BBC producer who now works as a communications professional at Google in Singapore, has come up with a personal mantra to help her remember to acknowledge the human factor of others and view every interaction as an opportunity for connection.

'I don't take a meeting, I make a friend', she says. This is one of her top tips for successfully collaborating across global teams, but not everyone supported this vision throughout her career.

> ***Early on in my career in television, a senior staffer pulled me aside and told me, 'You're extremely well liked, but you'll get the work done faster if you just put your head down and stop making friends.' At the time, this stung. I saw how those connections were the backbone for the team, motivating them on long overnight shoots far away from home, or to give that last hour of work after an exhausting day. I made a conscious decision to stick to my guns and not let go of this essential part of my toolkit.***

Years later, working at Google Singapore, she sees her approach paying off in clear ways, such as when she needs to wake up someone in the US in the middle of the night to address a potential public relations issue.

> ***In media relations, if I need to rely on a colleague in a different time zone to pick up the baton and communicate urgent information to a journalist, we need to trust one another. I try to forge a personal connection with everyone I work with regularly. I'm so glad I made that choice.***[13]

As an employee, you need to take your own connections seriously. A pre-COVID Stanford study in China showed that the performance of the home-based employee participants increased by 13 percent during the nine-month experiment, and attrition fell by 50 percent. But promotions conditional on performance appeared to fall by 50 percent. It seemed the old adage held true: out of sight, out of mind. As the study puts it:

> ***We heard anecdotal evidence for this from employees and managers during focus groups and interviews, and it was one factor that led some employees to return to the office to avoid what they perceived as a WFH promotion 'discrimination' penalty.***[14]

In a 2021 Joblist[15] survey of more than 1000 remote workers and managers, 95.5 per cent of managers said that remaining visible was a key to employee advancement. More than a third of the workers surveyed agreed. Some employees took steps to choreograph opportunities for connection by crafting a 'visibility strategy', which included doing things like taking on extra work for colleagues, checking in with co-workers often, volunteering for tasks or opportunities, keeping projects on deadline and being very detail oriented.

Managers in the Joblist survey noticed these extra efforts and viewed those employees as more motivated, productive and engaged. They were also more likely to reward these employees with promotions and raises.

When creating a visibility strategy for yourself, make sure you don't commit to overly taxing actions that will lead to burnout. You should be able to discuss your strategy with your boss and get input (especially if you're lucky enough to have a great boss like Rahul).

Create connection from afar

How can you create your own visibility strategy? Here are some ideas:

- Interact with colleagues on company networks like Slack.
- Attend virtual meetings with your camera on and speak up, especially about the successes of colleagues and those on your team.
- Offer new ideas and volunteer to take on projects that have a high likelihood of being seen by those above.
- Go into the office for meetings and social events when you can.
- Seek out video chats with colleagues outside work. Better yet, if you're in the same city, make social plans.

A good mindset to adopt is to remember that you are part of a team. As Kevin Eikenberry, a co-founder of the Remote Leadership Institute and co-author of *The Long-Distance Teammate* says,[16] 'If you think about your situation as "working from home," you're focusing on being insular and individual. What you really are is a remote teammate.'

In other words, you are an important part of a team of people working together in your city, region, country and world. Staying connected to these real human beings in intentional, empathetic, culturally sensitive ways is part of helping you, and them, rise and thrive.

Takeaways

- Let your thirst for adventure turbocharge your career. Remember that taking an overseas assignment can benefit you and your firm.
- Remove the 'r' from remote, as in emote. Emotional connection is key to success, especially when you don't see your colleagues, managers and/or employees in person every day.
- Acknowledge the human factor of dispersed workers by over-communicating, respecting time zone differences, and making more time for recognition than may seem necessary. (It's necessary.)
- Choreograph opportunities for connection when working far from team members and leaders.

Moving forward

This book is called *Don't Quit Your Day Job*, though plenty of people have obviously left positions. They've moved on, moved over, moved away. Movement is part of how you rise, and the opportunities within firms are growing more exciting, more diverse and, in many cases, more international.

Of course, plenty of people exit organisational life altogether, or never work within a firm in the first place. Many have full, vibrant and even thrilling careers and lives. I'm not saying all of those people must now go find a job in a firm. But for those of us who do choose to work within organisations – whether they be public or private – these attitudes and actions really can help.

For me, perseverance and optimism are perhaps the two traits I've relied on the most to help me rise and thrive. Other people have different primary strengths or identify more closely with other attributes: flexibility, openness, connection, movement. We all have amazing assets, many valuable 'tools' within us, and we live in a world with countless opportunities to develop these and build more. The *mindshifts* in the book are ways to help you do this.

Whichever of the preceding six chapters speaks to you and your situation the most, I hope you go forth with gusto and joy. The cheerleader in me will be shouting words of encouragement and support from the sidelines.

Acknowledgements

I would like to thank all of the people who have generously given their time and shared their stories for this book. While the book is partly drawn from my own experience and from research, its energy comes largely from all these amazing women and men I've met throughout my career. These are impressive, hardworking, thoughtful individuals who I've been fortunate to encounter. Thank you all for being willing to candidly share your tales.

I feel fortunate to have found Lucy Raymond and the global Wiley team, and am grateful for all their insights, work and support. Thank you CJ Wu for introducing me to Lucy and helping find this book a home. I could not have written this book without my co-writer, Wendy Paris. Thank you, Wendy, for endless hours on video conference and that one final week of working in person, with the unseasonably cold Santa Monica air coursing through the lobby of the Fairmont Hotel. Thanks to Christine Kenneally for introducing me to Wendy and helping make this book happen.

Thanks to all the people who have hired me over the years, the great leaders I've had (you know who you are) and the team members I've managed, especially those who were brave enough to offer a critique, helping me grow and pushing me closer to the 10-to-one critique-to-praise ratio Kim Scott recommends. Much thanks to my family for supporting me throughout my whole career and on this project – I'm especially proud of my sons, Zack and Jesse, who, having watched me over the years, expect to see women in leadership roles and in organisations and clubs, and speak out when that participation is lacking.

—Aliza Knox

Many thanks to Aliza Knox for giving me the chance to learn so much about how people rise and thrive within organisations, and to talk to her mentees and hear their inspiring stories. Throughout the process of working on this book, I'd find myself thinking, *Huh! That's what you're supposed to do at an organisation?! Who knew? I wish someone had told me that back in 1990 or 2010.* I am grateful for the opportunity to learn and help share these valuable insights with others.

Thanks to Chris Kenneally and Annie Murphy Paul for introducing me to Aliza, and to Lucy Raymond for her early, very astute articulation of what this book could offer to the conversation and how to best help it do that. A million thanks to Sharon Krum for pitching in at the last minute to help. Thanks to the experts who made themselves available to provide insight, and to everyone else who offered moral support and guidance including Wendy Hammers, Laura Rich, Abby Ellin, Joy Paris, Sidney Callahan, and my son, Alexander Paris-Callahan.

—Wendy Paris

Appendix: Quick reference guide

mindshift one: Go for both: Your work and your life are on the same team

- Your personal and professional life are on the same team. Move past the old mindset of 'my work OR my life.' Find synergies between them.
- Embrace your passions outside of work. Personal interests enliven you (and may help with your career in surprising ways).
- Have fun! Enjoying yourself at work supports camaraderie, commitment and creativity.
- Don't obsess about making the right choice. There is no 'one wrong decision' that will derail your career dreams. There are many routes to a fulfilling, successful life.
- Commit to a decision long enough to gain from it. Then, if it isn't where you want to be, 'iterate' — as in, make a change and move on.
- Opportunity + Action = Serendipity. Look for serendipity around you, and act on it.

mindshift two: Stamina is a muscle. Build yours!

- Perseverance + Enthusiasm = Stamina.
- Stamina is a career superpower that can be built. Put your energy into powering up yours.
- Self-care supports stamina. Adopt the mindshift that making time for family, friends and personal interests helps you keep going at work.
- Don't obsess about disappointments, rejections or failures; negative rumination saps stamina. Train your brain to obsess about your success.
- Remember that you always have options. You are not trapped. Do some job dating to remind you of this fact.
- Feeling totally responsible for disappointments – or big wins – saps stamina. Recognise that none of us has total control.

mindshift three: Connection trumps tech savvy...even in tech

- Amass that *other* critical capital, social capital – as in, genuine, trusting relationships and goodwill – throughout your career.
- Look for a few supportive, senior staff members to become 'sponsors' of your career and advocate for you within your firm. Sponsors are critical to rising and thriving in today's competitive work world.
- Assemble a personal board of directors outside your firm. Like companies, we all need a range of insights to help us grow.
- Mind your manners! Consideration is currency in today's often-dispersed, hyper-connected world. Small moves matter – thanking others, showing up, making good on commitments, and being present when you're with someone (rather than on your phone).

- Praise others often and in public (when they deserve it)
- Master the art of feedback – both giving it and getting it. Adopt the mindshift that receiving feedback is a tool for personal growth.

mindshift four: You are in a relationship with your career: Nurture it

- You are in a relationship with your career. It's your job to develop the best relationship you can over the years.
- Even a great career can't fulfil all your needs. Don't damage your career relationship by having unrealistic expectations of what a job can or 'should' do for you.
- Keep your eye on your prize – as in, recognise and pursue your goals. Don't wait around for someone else to notice your good work or hand you the promotion or opportunity you want. You have to identify your desires and go for them.
- Make sure your success gets seen. Practice the art of self-promotion with style.
- Fight back when wronged. Standing up for yourself can be hard to do, but it's part of maintaining a good relationship with your career.
- Set boundaries around work and personal life to get the most from both.

mindshift five: Get a move on! Use movement to stay energised and thrive

- Interests change; your career path can change with them. You are not locked into the industry, sector, job or location in which you began. Be open to new desires and pursue them.
- Prepare for your promotion, *then* ask. Demonstrating that you can do the job you desire helps your manager move you up.

- Be flexible and persistent when seeking a career change.
- Try to make one change at a time – instead of two or three – to facilitate movement.
- You can create momentum within your own firm or even within your job. Staying put does not have to mean languishing or being stuck.

mindshift six: Distant is the new diverse: Include the international and working-from-home team

- Let your thirst for adventure turbocharge your career. Remember that taking an overseas assignment can benefit you *and* your firm.
- Remove the 'r' from remote, as in *emote*. Emotional connection is key to success, especially when you don't see your colleagues, managers and/or employees in person every day.
- Acknowledge the human factor of dispersed workers by over-communicating, respecting time zone differences, and making more time for recognition than may seem necessary. (It's necessary.)
- Choreograph opportunities for connection when working far from team members and leaders.

Endnotes

LETTER TO THE READER

1. OECD 2017, 'Employment by enterprise size' (p. 42), *Entrepreneurship at a glance 2017*, OECD Publishing, Paris, https://doi.org/10.1787/entrepreneur_aag-2017-6-en.
2. Francis, T 2017, 'Why you probably work for a giant company, in 20 charts', *Wall Street Journal*, 6 April, https://www.wsj.com/graphics/big-companies-get-bigger/.
3. Krugman, P 2021, 'The revolt of the American worker', *The New York Times*, 14 October, https://www.nytimes.com/2021/10/14/opinion/workers-quitting-wages.html.
4. Noland, M, Moran, T, Kotschwar, B 2016, 'Is gender diversity profitable? Evidence from a global survey', Peterson Institute for International Economics, https://www.piie.com/publications/working-papers/gender-diversity-profitable-evidence-global-survey.

MINDSHIFT ONE: GO FOR BOTH: YOUR WORK AND YOUR LIFE ARE ON THE SAME TEAM

1. Anderson, C, Hunt, E 2018, 'New Zealand's Jacinda Ardern welcomes baby girl "to our village"', *The Guardian*, 21 June, https://www.theguardian.com/world/2018/jun/21/jacinda-ardern-new-zealand-prime-minister-birth-baby-girl.
2. Zoom Interview with Simon Kantor and Wendy Paris, 16 August 2021.

3. Slaughter, A-M 2012, 'Why women still can't have it all', *The Atlantic*, July/August, https://www.theatlantic.com/magazine/archive/2012/07/why-women-still-cant-have-it-all/309020/.
4. Zoom interview with Piruze Sabuncu and Wendy Paris, 6 July 2021.
5. Zoom interview with Art Markman and Wendy Paris, 2 June 2021.
6. Hartmans, A 2016. 'These 23 photos prove Google has the coolest offices around the world', *Business Insider*, 20 September, https://www.businessinsider.com/google-offices-around-the-world-photos-2016-9.
7. Paljug, K 2020, '16 cool job perks that keep employees happy', *Business News Daily*, 18 June, https://www.businessnewsdaily.com/5134-cool-job-benefits.html.
8. Olya, G 2020, '20 companies that let you bring your dog to work', Yahoo.com, 20 February, https://finance.yahoo.com/news/20-companies-let-bring-dog-090000585.html.
9. Jennings-Edquest, G 2021, 'The fine line between being friendly and friends with your boss', ABC Everyday, 19 January, https://www.abc.net.au/everyday/line-between-being-friendly-and-friends-with-your-boss/100006000.
10. Zoom interview with Emily Huo and Wendy Paris, 5 August 2021.
11. Phone interview with Emily Rubin and Wendy Paris, 9 December 2020.
12. Lutz, R, producer, 2018, *M.C. Escher: journey to infinity* (documentary), Ronin Films. Timbers, A, n.d. 'Art: Escher. The life of M.C. Escher', Brown University, http://www.math.brown.edu/tbanchof/Yale/project04/escherbio.html.
13. Zoom interview with Art Markman and Wendy Paris, 2 June 2021.
14. Hughes, C 2019, 'Expenditure on the production of television and film drama Australia by type 2019', Statista, 5 July, https://www.statista.com/statistics/954381/australia-expenditure-tv-film-drama-by-type/.

15. Phone interview with Sandra Barron and Wendy Paris, 20 May 2021.

MINDSHIFT TWO: STAMINA IS A MUSCLE. BUILD YOURS!

1. Ahrens, B 2021, 'Course 6202: Diversity and Cultural Competence', Ohio State School of Social Work.
2. Huffington, A. (2017, reprint). *The Sleep Revolution: Transforming Your Life, One Night at a Time*, Harmony, reprint edition. Pg. 9.
3 Phone interview with Glenn Geher and Wendy Paris, 29 June 2021.
4. Fredrickson, BL 2012, 'Updated thinking on positivity ratios', *American Psychologist*, vol. 68, no. 9, pp. 814–22; and, Fredrickson, BL 2013, *Love. 2.0: Finding Happiness and Health in Moments of Connection*, New York: Hudson Street Press; and Wadlinger, H. A., & Isaacowitz, D. M. 2006, 'Positive mood broadens visual attention to positive stimuli,' *Motivation and emotion*, 30(1), 87–99. https://doi.org/10.1007/s11031-006-9021-1.
5. Zoom interview with Marla Stone and Wendy Paris, 5 September 2021.
6. Zoom interview with Mariabrisa Olivares and Wendy Paris, 27 May 2021.
7. Nazar, J 2020, '12 Leadership lessons from DocuSign CEO Dan Springer', Entrepreneur.com, 18 November, https://www.entrepreneur.com/article/359416.

MINDSHIFT THREE: CONNECTION TRUMPS TECH SAVVY ... EVEN IN TECH

1. Zoom interview with Rahul Desai and Wendy Paris, 9 June 2021.
2. Beheshdi, N 2019, '10 timely statistics about the connection between employee engagement and wellness,' Forbes.com, 16 January, https://www.forbes.com/sites/nazbeheshti/2019/01/16/10-timely-statistics-about-the-connection-between-employee-engagement-and-wellness/?sh=1c60476222a0.
3. Phone interview. Annie Murphy Paul and Wendy Paris, 10 March 2021.

4. O'Boyle, E 2021, '4 things Gen Z and millennials expect from their workplace', Gallup.com, 30 March, https://www.gallup.com/workplace/336275/things-gen-millennials-expect-workplace.aspx.

5. Phone interview with Wendy Paris and Bala Subramaniam, 28 June 2021.

6. Ettlin, G 2021 'PSU study pinpoints workplace incivility, which is rising during the pandemic,' KGW8-TV, 2 August. KGW.com.

7. Phone interview with Amy Alkon and Wendy Paris, 27 August 2021.

8. Suttie, J, Marsh, J 2014, 'Is a happy life different from a meaningful one?', *Greater Good Magazine*, 25 February, https://greatergood.berkeley.edu/article/item/happy_life_different_from_meaningful_life. Zhang, D, Chan, DC-C, Niu, L, Zou, D, Chan, AT-Y, Gao, TT, Zhong, B, Sit, RW-S, Wong, SY-S 2018, 'Meaning and its association with happiness, health and healthcare utilization: a cross sectional study', *Journal of Affective Disorders*, vol 227, pp 795-802.

9. Alkon, A 2014, *Good Manners for Nice People Who Sometimes Say F*ck*, St Martin's Press, New York.

10. Rogers, T, Milkman KL, John, LK, Norton, MI 2015, 'Beyond good intentions: prompting people to make plans improves follow-through on important tasks', *Behavioral Science & Policy*, vol. 1, no. 2, p. 33–41.

11. Stanborough, J 2019, 'How to tell if you could be addicted to your phone', healthline.com, 17 October, https://www.healthline.com/health/mental-health/cell-phone-addiction.

12. Scott, K 2021, 'A thought on praise: criticism ratios' [LinkedIn] November.

MINDSHIFT FOUR: YOU ARE IN A RELATIONSHIP WITH YOUR CAREER: NURTURE IT

1. Neal, B 2021, Radical candor: Podcast season 3, episode 9: The problem with passion. Available from: https://www.radicalcandor.com/podcast/problem-with-passion-podcast/.

2. Telephone interview with Emily Rubin and Wendy Paris, 9 December 2020.
3. Pellegrino, J 2021, 'It has been an intense, but extraordinarily rewarding 3 years. . .' [LinkedIn], September.
4. Zoom interview with Cindy Carpenter and Aliza Knox, 19 August 2021.
5. Warrell, M 2019, 'Train the brave', https://margiewarrell.com/train-the-brave-3/. Blog post, March 19, 2019.
6. Lakhani, N 2020, "I'll be fierce for all of us": Deb Haaland on climate, Native Rights and Biden', *The Guardian*, 27 December, https://www.theguardian.com/environment/2020/dec/27/deb-haaland-interview-interior-secretary-native-americans.
7. Goldwin, C 2021, *Career and family: women's century-long journey toward equity*, Princeton University Press. Pg. 213.
8. Hunt, E 2021, '"It just doesn't stop!" Do we need a new law to ban out-of-hours emails?', *The Guardian*, 29 June, https://www.theguardian.com/money/2021/jun/29/it-just-doesnt-stop-do-we-need-a-new-law-to-ban-out-of-hours-emails. Keane, J 2021, 'The legal right to disconnect could become the norm in Europe', CNBC, 22 June, https://www.cnbc.com/2021/06/22/right-to-disconnect-could-become-the-norm-in-europe.html. Henshall, A 2021, 'Can the "right to disconnect" exist in a remote-work world?', BBC, 21 May, https://www.bbc.com/worklife/article/20210517-can-the-right-to-disconnect-exist-in-a-remote-work-world.
9. Zoom call with Wendy Paris, 20 May 2021.

MINDSHIFT FIVE: GET A MOVE ON! USE MOVEMENT TO STAY ENERGISED AND THRIVE

1. Zoom interview with Lisa Wang and Wendy Paris, 1 August 2021.
2. Ashworth-Keppel, T 2018, 'Changing jobs: how often is too often?' Australian Institute of Business, 24 July, https://www.aib.edu.au/blog/career-development/changing-jobs-how-often-is-too-often/.

3. US Bureau of Labor Statistics 2020, 'Employee tenure summary', US Bureau of Labor Statistics, September 22, https://www.bls.gov/news.release/tenure.nr0.htm.
4. Kolmar, C 2021, 'Average number of jobs in a lifetime [2021]: All Statistics', Zippia: The Career Expert, 19 May, https://www.zippia.com/advice/average-number-jobs-in-lifetime/.
5. Wittenberg-Cox, A 2019, 'Linking gender and generational balance: careers in the age of longevity', Forbes, 29 June, https://www.forbes.com/sites/avivahwittenbergcox/2019/06/29/linking-gender-generational-balance-careers-in-the-age-of-longevity/?sh=6c0b1d351f1d.
6. Zoom interview with Simon Kantor and Wendy Paris, 16 August 2021.
7. AIB Blog 2018, 'How to get promoted at every level', Australian Institute of Business, 21 February, https://www.aib.edu.au/blog/career-development/how-to-get-promoted-at-every-level/.
8. Zoom interview with Sue Shilbury and Aliza Knox, 5 October 2021.
9. Zoom interview with Simon Kantor and Wendy Paris, 16 August 2021.
10. Neisloss, L 2021, '"I'm not going back": a Boston therapist changes careers for her own mental health', GBH.com, October 21, 2021.
11. Email interview with Erfi Anugrah and Aliza Knox, 2 April 2021.
12. Zoom interview with Korin Kohen and Wendy Paris, 19 August 2021.
13. Grant, A 2021, 'There's a name for the blah you're feeling: it's called languishing', *The New York Times*, 19 April, https://www.nytimes.com/2021/04/19/well/mind/covid-mental-health-languishing.html.
14. Laker, B, Patel C, Budhwar P, Malik A 2020, 'How job crafting can make work more satisfying', MIT Sloan Management Review, 17 September, https://sloanreview.mit.edu/article/how-job-crafting-can-make-work-more-satisfying/.

MINDSHIFT SIX: DISTANT IS THE NEW DIVERSE: INCLUDE THE INTERNATIONAL AND WORKING-FROM-HOME TEAM

1. Zoom call with Sierra Dasso and Wendy Paris, 20 May 2021.
2. Lorenzo, R, Voigt, N, Tsusaka, M, Krentz, M, Abouzahr, K 2018, 'How diverse leadership teams boost innovation', Boston Consulting Group, 23 January, https://www.bcg.com/en-au/publications/2018/how-diverse-leadership-teams-boost-innovation.
3. Phone interview with Malini Vaidya and Aliza Knox, 18 August 2021
4. Brown-Philpot, S n.d., Lean in stories, https://leanin.org/stories/stacy-brown-philpot#.
5. Gelles, D 2018, 'Stacy Brown-Philpot of TaskRabbit on being a Black woman in Silicon Valley', 13 July, https://www.nytimes.com/2018/07/13/business/stacy-brown-philpot-taskrabbit-corner-office.html.
6. Google Hangouts interview with Crystal Hayling and Wendy Paris, 27 August 2021.
7. Interview with Drew Sanocki and Wendy Paris, 17 July 2021, Santa Monica, California.
8. Google Hangouts interview with Kate Fleming and Wendy Paris, 14 July 2021.
9. Google Hangouts interview with Korin Kohen and Wendy Paris, 19 August 2021.
10. Zoom interview with Korin Kohen and Wendy Paris, 19 August 2021.
11. Maxfield, B 2020, 'The collapse of social capital: Ignoring the cultural impact of WFH will erode relationships and results', 27 October, https://cruciallearning.com/press/work-from-home-and-the-collapse-of-social-capital-ignoring-the-cultural-impact-of-wfh-will-erode-relationships-and-results/.
12. Private email correspondence.
13. Phone call with Batsheva Lazarus and Aliza Knox, 22 September 2021.

14. Bloom, N, Liang, J, Roberts, J, Ying, ZJ 2015, 'Does working from home work? Evidence from a Chinese experiment', *Quarterly Journal of Economics*, February, vol. 130, issue 1, pp. 1650218.

15. Joblist 2021, 'Getting yourself noticed as an employee working remotely', Joblist, 7 January, https://www.joblist.com/trends/getting-yourself-noticed-as-an-employee-working-remotely.

16. Vozza, S 2021, 'How to remain visible to your boss when you work remotely', Fast Company, 10 March, https://www.fastcompany.com/90612136/how-to-remain-visible-to-your-boss-when-you-work-remotely.

Index